BURN THE MYTHS, NOT YOUR DINNER

A Hilarious Guide to Healthy Cooking
Without the Nonsense

UDIT LEKHI

ISBN
Paperback 979-8-89632-473-7
Hardcase 979-8-89632-953-4

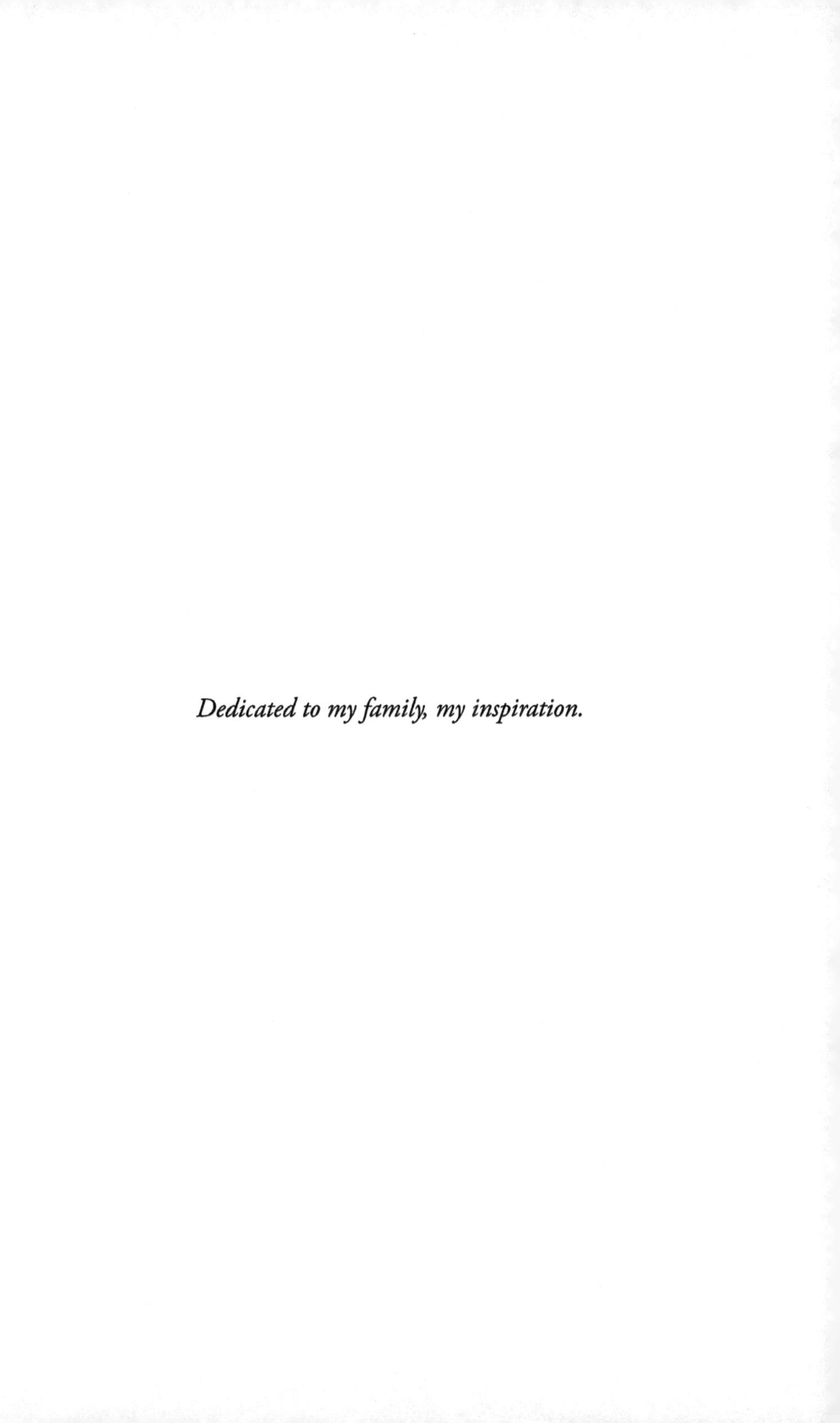

Dedicated to my family, my inspiration.

Contents

Preface 7

Introduction 9

PART I: GETTING REAL WITH INGREDIENTS

1. From Farm to Fibs – What 'Fresh' Really
    Means at the Grocery Store 15

2. Non-Stick Nonsense – Why Your Cookware
    Might Be Plotting Against You 45

3. The Oil Slick – Choosing Fats That Won't
    Let You Down 79

PART II: RECLAIMING YOUR KITCHEN

4. Nostalgic Carbs – Making Classics Like Pasta,
    Paneer, and Parathas Healthier .115

5. Food Fads & Fibs – Debunking Ridiculous
    Health Claims 129

PART III: BUILDING A SUSTAINABLE, JOYFUL RELATIONSHIP WITH FOOD

6. Building a Healthier Relationship with Food 143

7. The Spice Route – Reclaiming the
    Indian Masala Shelf 151

8. Cooking the Indian Way – Rediscovering
    Ancestral Techniques 161

9. Sweet Satisfaction – Desserts That
    Won't Sabotage Your Health 179

PART IV: FINAL REFLECTIONS

10. Epilogue: Cooking with Confidence and Joy 191

Acknowledgments, References and Resources 195

Acknowledgments 201

From Baking Blunders to Kitchen Boss

Let me tell you how this whole cooking thing started. At first, it had nothing to do with healthy eating—it was entirely about impressing my wife. Yes, you read that right. Baking was my first battlefield, mostly because she has a weakness for anything sweet. I thought, "How hard can it be to bake?" Apron tied, flour flying, and an oven that seemed more like a fire hazard than a tool—I was set. My first cake? A complete science experiment gone wrong. But hey, she didn't leave me, so I consider it a victory.

Then came the ambitious leap to Thai food, her absolute favourite. I remember wandering the grocery store, clueless, looking for tamarind paste and kaffir lime leaves. After a few tries (and one too-salty disaster), I finally managed a curry that didn't immediately send her running for the takeout menu. Mission accomplished.

But the stakes rose higher when our daughter came along. Suddenly, I was tackling pasta, baked treats, and the never-ending requests for snacks. Every time I cooked something new, my mini food critic would take one skeptical look and say, "Nice try, Dad, but where's the pizza?" In those moments, I realized my cooking wasn't just about taste; it was about making food that brought joy to my family's table. Little did I know, those burnt cakes, and salty curries were the foundation of a journey that would lead me beyond taste to something even more rewarding: cooking that brings both joy and nourishment to the table.

What started as a fun way to impress my wife and appease my daughter slowly evolved into something bigger. Healthy cooking was never my goal, but the more I learned, the more I realized how many ridiculous fads are out there. You know the ones: that magical powder claiming to detox your soul, or the absurdly priced granola that promises to melt away 10 pounds just by looking at it. It didn't take long to understand that "health" in the food industry often means more hype than actual benefit. That realization—the gap between the hype and the truth—sparked an idea: what if healthy cooking didn't have to mean compromises or confusion? What if it could be joyful, simple, and real?

So, here we are. This book isn't about giving up everything you love and replacing it with kale and quinoa. It's about real food that tastes good without the nonsense. Small changes that make a big difference, but don't make you wish you were munching on cardboard.

I've made plenty of cooking mistakes (believe me, we'll get to those), but I've also figured out how to balance flavour, health, and even a little fun along the way. We're going to dive into everything from choosing cookware that won't sabotage your meal to laughing off the latest food fads. And yes, there will be some quirky, spice-laden anecdotes from our household experiments—because isn't food all about stories, too?

If you've ever burned a dish, fallen for a food fad, or wondered if healthy food could still taste indulgent, you're in the right place. Let's cook without the nonsense and bring back the joy of real food.

Introduction

Healthy Cooking – It's Not a Detox, It's Dinner

Let's get one thing straight—healthy cooking isn't about depriving yourself or forcing down sad salads and green juices that taste like grass. Nope. In my house, healthy means delicious, hearty, and packed with flavour.

I started off by trying to impress my family with baked treats and exotic dishes, but eventually, I realized I needed to figure out how to make those meals healthier without compromising on taste. That's when I stumbled into the confusing world of "health food" marketing. You know, those brands that slap "natural" on their products, jack up the price, and make you feel like you're buying bottled miracles? Yeah, they got me too. Turns out, half the stuff marketed as healthy is basically expensive nonsense.

Healthy Cooking: The Journey from Marketing Myths to Family Traditions

Here's the thing—healthy cooking isn't about buying every superfood or obsessing over the latest diet trends. It's about balance, real ingredients, and food that doesn't make you want to run back to pizza delivery. I learned this the hard way, but hey, that's why you don't have to.

The real turning point came thanks to my wife, who's Pahadi (from the Himalayas), with an entirely different food heritage from my own Punjabi roots. She introduced me to local ingredients that were simple, earthy, and packed with flavour—fresh greens, millet, and dal (lentils). These foods weren't trendy; they were staples she grew up with. Watching her cook with these ingredients reminded me that good food didn't need a "superfood" label to be healthy or a hefty price tag to be delicious. Her Pahadi roots taught me the beauty of simple, wholesome cooking—dishes rooted in tradition, not trends. It was a reminder that food doesn't need a superfood label to be healthy.

As I learned from her, I started blending those earthy, wholesome Pahadi Flavors with my own Punjabi love for spice and let's be real, butter. Together, we figured out how to make meals that felt like an indulgence yet were nourishing and balanced. There's something grounding about cooking with ingredients that have stood the test of time, passed down through families, rather than chasing the next big health fad.

The Superfood Reality Check

Not that I didn't try the superfood route. There was a phase where I loaded our pantry with anything that promised health benefits. I once bought an expensive "superfood blend" that supposedly boosted energy, clarity, and maybe even confidence. One taste, and I was convinced I'd paid ₹1,500 for glorified nimbu pani (lemon water). Meanwhile, my daughter sat across the table, happily enjoying dal chawal (lentils and rice) with a dollop of ghee (clarified butter), and I had to laugh. Here was my "superfood" right in front of me, a dish that had been nourishing families for generations without any fanfare.

That was my wake-up call. Real healthy cooking isn't about what's trending. It's about what sustains you, what tastes good, and what's practical enough to make every day.

The fancy label might have promised miracles, but I was left with a lemon-water reality check and an overpriced powder gathering dust on my shelf. Lesson learned: sometimes the most nutritious meal is already on your plate.

Why This Book is Different

This book isn't here to tell you to replace all your favourite foods with kale and quinoa. It's about getting back to basics, choosing ingredients thoughtfully, and making healthy cooking something you look forward to. I've done the trial and error, so you don't have to.

We're going to cut through the hype and focus on what truly makes food good for you. This book will help you spot fake health claims, avoid the food fads that complicate your life, and make small changes that add up over time. You don't need a pantry full of "superfoods" or a blender that costs more than your rent. What you need is a few good ingredients, a sense of adventure, and a little humour.

Healthy cooking isn't about deprivation or pretence—it's about reclaiming the joy of eating and making every meal count. Let's skip the nonsense and get started.

PART I

Getting Real with Ingredients

Chapter 1

From Farm to Fibs – What 'Fresh' Really Means at the Grocery Store

Supermarkets vs. Reality

The Shiny Facade

Supermarkets are a wonderland of perfection—or so they'd like you to believe. Every fruit gleam like it's been prepped for a jewellery ad, and every vegetable looks like it's straight out of a food magazine. But let's peel back this glossy facade and dive into the reality beneath all that shine. What's on display isn't just produce—it's a carefully curated performance, complete with props and special effects.

Take apples, for instance. Those impossibly shiny, flawless apples weren't picked off a tree looking that way. They've been waxed, buffed, and polished like a pair of vintage shoes. This wax coating does more than just catch your eye—it traps moisture, delays ripening, and extends shelf life. Sounds good on paper, right? Except that wax also traps any residual pesticides or dirt, leaving you biting into a fruit that's more spa-treated than sun-kissed. It's like eating the apple equivalent of an over-contoured Instagram influencer—beautiful, but a little unnatural.

And then there's the humble cucumber. Have you ever wondered why the ones in supermarkets come shrink-wrapped in plastic? It's not because cucumbers need protection from the elements—it's because supermarkets have realized that shiny plastic sells better. A plastic-wrapped cucumber looks clean, professional, and ready for business. In contrast, the ones you find at your local sabzi mandi (vegetable market) might have a speck of dirt on them, but at least they feel alive—like they just leapt off the vine and into your shopping bag.

The illusion doesn't stop at waxing and wrapping. Supermarkets are masters of the misting machine. You've seen it: a fine spray of water over leafy greens, giving them a dewy, just-picked look. It's refreshing, sure, but it's also deceptive. That mist is purely aesthetic—those greens weren't freshly plucked from a field; they've been sitting in cold storage for weeks. The water is a quick pick-me-up for tired spinach and coriander, but as soon as you bring them home, they'll wilt faster than your enthusiasm for eating healthy.

Speaking of cold storage, let's talk about the secret life of supermarket produce. Ever wonder how apples are available year-round, or why tomatoes look perfect in winter? It's because they've been through a time-traveling journey that involves months—sometimes up to a year—in cold storage. Fruits like apples are picked before they're ripe and stored in low-oxygen chambers to delay aging. By the time they hit the shelves, they're still "technically" fresh, but the flavour and nutrients have taken a backseat. Imagine meeting someone who's been cryogenically frozen for decades—they might look great, but you can tell something's a little off.

Tomatoes have their own story. These supermarket darlings are often plucked green and gassed with ethylene to turn them red. This process, known as artificial ripening, doesn't let the tomato develop its natural sweetness or flavour—it's like painting a house to hide cracks in the wall. Sure, the tomato looks the part, but bite into it, and you're met with a bland, watery disappointment. Compare that to the sun-ripened, slightly misshapen tomatoes at your local market, and there's no contest.

And let's not forget bananas—the drama queens of the fruit world. Naturally, bananas develop brown spots as they ripen, a sign that they're at their sweetest. But supermarkets don't want you to see that. Instead, bananas are treated and refrigerated to maintain their uniform yellow colour for as long as possible. It's like putting them in a beauty pageant where spots are grounds for disqualification. But the joke's on us when we realize those "perfect" bananas taste like chalk compared to the spotty ones your dadi (grandmother) would swear by.

Supermarkets have turned food into a theatre, and we're the audience falling for the spectacle. But the problem with all this perfection is that it's changing the way we think about produce. We've been trained to equate shininess with quality, straightness with superiority, and uniformity with freshness. Crooked carrots, lumpy potatoes, and apples with a few scars are seen as "inferior," even though they often taste better than their over-polished counterparts.

This obsession with appearances has created a demand for produce that looks good, even if it compromises on flavour, nutrition, and authenticity. Take lettuce, for example. At a mandi, it might look a little rough around the edges, but it has that earthy, fresh-from-the-ground smell. In contrast, supermarket lettuce is all show—crisp on the outside but often flavourless. It's the difference between a home-cooked meal and a microwave dinner. One is real, imperfect, and bursting with personality; the other is mass-produced and soulless.

The worst part? This drive for perfection creates mountains of waste. Fruits and vegetables that don't meet supermarket standards are rejected and discarded, even though they're perfectly edible. Imagine all the lumpy carrots, scarred tomatoes, and spotty bananas that never make it to your cart because they didn't pass the "beauty test." It's not just a waste of food—it's a waste of the resources, water, and labour that went into growing them.

What's even sadder is how this illusion of perfection changes the way we shop. Instead of using our senses to pick fruits and vegetables—smelling, touching, and even listening for that perfect watermelon thud—we rely on superficial cues. We're drawn to the shiny, the straight, and the symmetrical, even though these qualities have little to do with taste or nutrition.

Supermarkets have convinced us that food should look flawless, but real food isn't perfect. Real food has quirks, scars, and stories. It's the twisted carrot that grew around a rock, the apple with a bruise because it fell from a tree, and the tomato that's slightly wrinkled because it ripened in the sun. These are the foods that taste like they belong to the earth—not a factory.

At the end of the day, the shiny facade of supermarkets is just that—a facade. The apples, cucumbers, and tomatoes on display may look perfect, but they've been through more treatments than a Bollywood star prepping for an award show. Behind all that shine is a reality that's far less glamorous and far more wasteful.

So, the next time you're at a supermarket, take a moment to see through the illusion. Look past the wax, the mist, and the lighting, and remember that food doesn't have to be flawless to be fantastic. Because in the end, the quirkiest carrot and the lumpiest tomato often have the most flavour—and the best stories to tell.

Psychological Traps

Supermarkets may look innocent, but they're psychological battlegrounds where your willpower faces a series of expertly designed traps. From the moment you walk in, you're nudged, prodded, and subtly influenced into buying more than you need and often things you didn't even plan to buy. It's like entering a game of chess, except you're playing against an opponent who knows your every move.

Let's start with the layout. Ever noticed how essentials like milk, bread, and sugar are always at the farthest corners of the store? That's no accident. Supermarkets make you walk through aisles of snacks, biscuits, and beverages to get to your basics, hoping you'll pick up a few impulse items along the way. It's like navigating a maze where the reward for finding the exit is an overflowing cart of goodies you didn't intend to buy. By the time you've reached the milk section, you're holding three packets of namkeen (savoury snacks), two bottles of soda, and that fancy brand of pasta that was never on your list.

And then there's the eye-level trick. Supermarkets know that items placed at eye level are more likely to end up in your cart, so that's where they display the pricier, premium products. Cheaper, store-brand options are tucked away on the bottom shelves, forcing you to squat or stretch to find them. Take rice, for example. The ₹2,000-per-kg Basmati is proudly displayed at eye level, while the perfectly decent ₹100-per-kg option is hidden near your feet. It's a psychological nudge that makes spending more feel almost automatic.

The lighting is another weapon in the supermarket arsenal. Soft, warm lights are strategically placed to make fruits and vegetables gleam like jewels. Tomatoes glow redder, bananas look sunnier, and cucumbers seem crisper under this flattering illumination. It's the same trick that restaurants use to make their food look irresistible—except here, it's convincing you that a perfectly ordinary potato is a premium purchase. Back home, under your kitchen light, those same tomatoes suddenly look a little less vibrant and a lot more ordinary.

Music is another sneaky trick. Have you ever noticed how supermarkets play slow, calming tunes? It's not to make your shopping experience more enjoyable—it's to slow you down. Studies show that slower music encourages shoppers to linger longer, increasing the likelihood of impulse purchases. You might find yourself absentmindedly browsing the aisles, humming along to a nostalgic tune, and tossing an extra packet of biscuits into your cart. It's like being hypnotized into shopping.

Then there's the bakery section. Ever wondered why the smell of freshly baked bread seems to follow you everywhere in a supermarket? That's not just the aroma of actual bread—it's strategically released scents designed to make you feel hungry and nostalgic. That comforting smell of warm bread isn't just reminding you of your dadi's (grandmother's) homemade parathas (Indian flatbread); it's nudging you toward buying an expensive artisanal loaf that you probably don't need. You're not just buying bread—you're buying a feeling.

Supermarkets are also experts at creating a sense of scarcity. Ever noticed those signs that say, "Limited Stock" or "Hurry, Only 3 Left!"? They're designed to trigger FOMO (fear of missing out). Even if you weren't planning to buy a fancy olive oil, that little note makes you think, "What if I need this later?" Before you know it, the bottle is in your cart, along with a vague sense of accomplishment for snagging something "exclusive."

Discounts are another classic trap. Who hasn't fallen for a "Buy One, Get One Free" deal? It sounds like a no-brainer—you're getting more for less! But here's the catch: most of the time, you didn't need the first item, let alone the second one. Suddenly, you have two jars of mayonnaise sitting in your pantry and no idea how you're going to finish them before they expire. The same goes for combo deals: you didn't plan to buy an extra bottle of ketchup, but hey, it was only ₹50 more.

Even the labels are designed to manipulate you. Words like "farm fresh," "handpicked," and "organic" create a halo of health and quality around products, even when they don't necessarily deserve it. Take "farm fresh." It sounds wholesome, but what does it really mean? Did someone pick those tomatoes at dawn and rush them straight to the store? Probably not. It's just a phrase designed to evoke an image of rustic authenticity, tricking you into paying a premium for produce that's no fresher than what your sabziwala (local vegetable vendor) sells.

And don't even get me started on the checkout counter. This final frontier is a masterstroke of psychological manipulation. Small shelves near the billing area are loaded with chocolates, gum, and tiny snack packs. By the time you've reached the counter, you're tired, bored, and vulnerable. That ₹20 Dairy Milk bar suddenly seems like a great idea. You grab it, convincing yourself it's a small treat for surviving the ordeal of grocery shopping. Multiply that by hundreds of customers, and those tiny treats add up to a significant chunk of the supermarket's revenue.

The tragedy of all these psychological tricks is that they shift our focus away from what truly matters. Instead of picking produce based on smell, texture, and flavour, we're drawn to shiny labels, sleek packaging, and clever marketing. We start valuing appearance over substance, convenience over authenticity, and price over quality.

But the truth is, real food doesn't need tricks to win you over. Think about the mangoes you buy from your local mandi (vegetable market). They might not be perfectly uniform in size, but their smell alone can transport you to summer afternoons spent devouring the fruit straight off the seed. Or the crooked carrots from the sabziwala (local vegetable vendor)—they might look quirky, but they're bursting with flavour in a way that mass-produced supermarket carrots can't match.

Supermarkets might excel at manipulation, but they can't replicate the authenticity of food that's grown with care and sold with pride. The next time you're tempted by a "limited edition" snack or a perfectly polished apple, remember that these tricks are just that—tricks. True freshness and flavour aren't found under fluorescent lights; they're found in the imperfections, quirks, and stories that real food carries with it.

Imperfect Yet Irreplaceable

Let's talk about the underdogs of the produce world—the crooked carrots, scarred tomatoes, and slightly lopsided apples. These are the fruits and vegetables that don't fit the supermarket mold of perfection. They're the ones that grow a little differently, with quirks that reflect their natural environment. And yet, they're cast aside like uninvited guests at a fancy dinner party. In the age of airbrushed apples and waxed cucumbers, imperfection has become a crime— but it's time we changed that.

Imagine a world where tomatoes didn't have to be perfectly round, where a carrot could grow as curly as it liked, and where bananas with brown spots were celebrated instead of sidelined. That world isn't a utopia—it's your local mandi (vegetable market). Here, produce comes with a story, not a script. The slightly bruised mango isn't a reject; it's a testimony to its journey from the tree to your hands. That crooked cucumber didn't grow in a factory—it thrived in the earth, embracing its quirks along the way.

Supermarkets, on the other hand, have declared war on imperfection. Anything that doesn't conform to their rigid standards is rejected, discarded, or downgraded. It's not because these fruits and vegetables lack flavour or nutrition—in fact, it's often the opposite. Imperfect produce is usually just as delicious, if not more so, than its picture-perfect counterparts. But in a world obsessed with aesthetics, looking the part has become more important than playing it.

Take the humble carrot. In a supermarket, you'll only find perfectly straight, evenly coloured specimens, all arranged like soldiers in a lineup. But have you ever tasted a carrot that grew in the wild, twisting and turning around rocks and roots? It's sweeter, richer, and full of character. That carrot didn't just survive—it thrived. It's the vegetable equivalent of a self-made entrepreneur, and yet it's rejected because it doesn't "fit the mold."

Tomatoes, too, face this discrimination. The ones in supermarkets are bred for uniformity, picked green, and artificially ripened to achieve that ideal shade of red. But bite into one, and you're greeted with a bland, watery flavour that's more cardboard than culinary. Now compare that to a sun-ripened, slightly scarred tomato from your local sabziwala (vegetable vendor). Its skin might be a little rough, but its taste is a symphony of sweetness, acidity, and earthiness. It's the kind of tomato that makes you want to cook a fresh batch of chutney or toss it straight into a curry.

This obsession with perfection doesn't just affect our shopping habits—it affects the entire food system. Farmers are forced to discard huge amounts of produce simply because it doesn't meet supermarket standards. Studies show that up to 40% of fruits and vegetables are wasted before they even reach the shelves, not because they're inedible, but because they don't look the part. Imagine all the lumpy potatoes, scarred apples, and bumpy cucumbers that never get a chance to shine. It's a tragedy of wasted flavour, nutrition, and effort.

The irony is that imperfect produce often has a lot to offer. The same quirks that supermarkets reject are often signs of resilience and character. A mango with a scar on its skin might have survived a monsoon, soaking up nutrients that give it an intense, complex flavour. A crooked carrot might have navigated rocky soil, developing a sweetness that straight ones can't match. Imperfection isn't a flaw—it's a badge of honour.

In fact, some of the best meals are made from the quirkiest ingredients. Think of a hearty sabzi (vegetable curry) made with slightly overripe tomatoes, or a bharta (mashed dish) made with the wonkiest brinjals (eggplants). These dishes don't demand perfection—they thrive on personality. It's the kind of cooking that feels authentic, rooted, and deeply satisfying. When you use imperfect produce, you're not just making a meal—you're telling a story.

The beauty of imperfection isn't just in the flavour—it's in the joy of embracing food as it is, not as it "should" be. It's in choosing the lumpy tomato because it smells amazing, or the slightly wrinkled apple because it feels heavy with juice. It's about trusting your senses, not just your eyes, to guide your choices. And it's about reconnecting with the essence of food—its taste, texture, and aroma—without being blinded by appearances.

But here's the kicker: embracing imperfect produce isn't just good for your taste buds—it's good for the planet. When we reject fruits and vegetables for their looks, we're contributing to a culture of waste. All those rejected carrots, potatoes, and apples don't just disappear—they're thrown away, often in staggering quantities. This waste represents not just lost food, but also wasted water, energy, and resources. By choosing imperfect produce, we're taking a stand against this wasteful system and supporting a more sustainable way of eating.

Local markets are a haven for imperfect produce. Here, you'll find tomatoes with uneven shapes, mangoes with sunspots, and cucumbers with a bend or two. These aren't flaws—they're reminders that food is grown, not manufactured. Shopping at a mandi is like stepping into a world where imperfection is celebrated, not punished. It's a place where you can haggle over prices, chat with vendors, and pick produce with your hands, your nose, and your heart.

Imagine this: you're at your local mandi, and you spot a pile of slightly bruised guavas. The vendor, an old-timer who knows his fruit like a poet knows his verses, smiles at you and says, "Madam, these are the sweetest guavas you'll ever taste. Try one." You take a bite, and he's right—the flavour explodes in your mouth, a perfect balance of sweet and tangy. It's a reminder that true quality isn't about looks—it's about experience.

So, the next time you're shopping for groceries, skip the shiny facade of the supermarket and head to your local mandi. Embrace the lumpy, the crooked, and the scarred. These aren't imperfections—they're stories waiting to be tasted.

Environmental Aftermath

The consequences of our obsession with flawless produce stretch far beyond what we see in the aisles of a supermarket. Beneath the glossy surface lies a far grittier story—one of waste, pollution, and environmental damage that's anything but picture-perfect. Every time we reject a slightly crooked carrot or a banana with a brown spot, we're contributing to a food system that prioritizes aesthetics over sustainability and substance.

Start with food waste, the silent but staggering consequence of our obsession with perfection. Globally, an estimated 1.3 billion tonnes of food are wasted every year, and much of this comes from fruits and vegetables that never make it past the farm gate. In India, where resources like water and land are precious commodities, the sight of perfectly edible but "ugly" produce being discarded feels particularly jarring. Farmers are forced to abandon mountains of carrots, potatoes, and tomatoes that don't meet supermarket standards, even though these quirks have no impact on taste or nutrition. It's like judging a novel by its font instead of its content.

And where does this wasted food go? Often, it ends up in landfills, where it decomposes and releases methane—a greenhouse gas far more potent than carbon dioxide. That quirky potato you left behind because it had a spot. Its journey might end with it sitting in a heap of rotting food, contributing to climate change instead of becoming part of a delicious aloo matar (potato and pea curry). What a waste of potential—and of flavour.

Then there's the environmental cost of plastic packaging. Supermarkets wrap produce in layers of plastic to make it look clean, convenient, and appealing. But let's call it what it is: a problem disguised as a solution. That cling-wrapped cucumber might seem harmless in your cart, but its packaging will outlive you, your children, and probably the cucumber's descendants. Once discarded, this plastic enters our oceans, our soil, and eventually our food chain, creating a cycle of harm that's hard to escape.

Compare this to your local mandi (vegetable market), where the sabziwala (vegetable vendor) hands your vegetables wrapped in nothing but yesterday's newspaper. No frills, no waste, just practical, eco-friendly charm. It's a reminder that freshness doesn't need to come with a side of environmental guilt.

The problem isn't just about packaging—it's also about transportation. Supermarkets rely on massive supply chains to ensure that you can have apples in summer and mangoes in winter, regardless of what nature intended. This means that much of the produce you see has travelled thousands of kilometres, leaving a trail of carbon emissions in its wake. That "farm-fresh" label on a supermarket tomato? It probably took a long-haul flight to get to your plate. Meanwhile, the tomato at your local mandi might have come from a farm just a few kilometres away, its journey leaving behind nothing but a trail of earthy footprints.

The irony is that our quest for "perfection" is ruining the very earth that provides for us. Growing picture-perfect produce often requires excessive use of water, pesticides, and fertilizers—all to meet arbitrary beauty standards. These chemicals seep into our soil and water, damaging ecosystems and threatening biodiversity. All so we can have shiny apples and uniform cucumbers that, frankly, taste no better than their "imperfect" cousins.

The good news? It doesn't have to be this way. By making small changes to how we shop and what we value, we can turn the tide on this environmental aftermath. Start by embracing imperfect produce. That crooked carrot or lumpy tomato isn't just a quirky addition to your plate—it's a statement against waste and for sustainability. Choosing these underdogs is a way of saying, "I care about flavour, not flair."

Supporting local farmers and markets is another way to reduce your environmental footprint. When you buy produce from a nearby farm or mandi, you're not just getting fresher, tastier food—you're also cutting down on the emissions generated by transporting out-of-season fruits and vegetables halfway across the globe. Plus, local markets often use minimal or no packaging, reducing the amount of waste you take home.

And let's talk about seasonality. Eating seasonal produce isn't just better for your health—it's better for the planet. Seasonal fruits and vegetables don't require the artificial interventions—like cold storage, forced ripening, or long-distance shipping—that out-of-season produce does. They're nature's way of providing exactly what we need, when we need it. In summer, you get hydrating fruits like watermelon and cucumbers; in winter, you get warming greens and root vegetables. It's a delicious, sustainable cycle that supermarkets often disrupt in their bid to offer "everything, all the time."

Making these changes doesn't mean swearing off supermarkets or going full zero-waste overnight. It's about small, meaningful shifts in how we think about food. It's about appreciating the effort and resources that go into growing produce, and choosing options that honour that effort rather than waste it. It's about saying no to plastic-wrapped cucumbers and yes to newspaper-wrapped vegetables. It's about valuing the crooked carrot as much as the straight one.

The environmental aftermath of our obsession with perfect produce is a problem of our own making, but it's one we can solve together. By choosing local, seasonal, and imperfect food, we're not just saving resources and reducing waste—we're reconnecting with the earth, our communities, and the simple joy of eating food as it was meant to be.

Because at the end of the day, isn't it better to eat a crooked carrot that tastes amazing than a perfect one that's travelled halfway around the world to disappoint you? The planet would certainly agree.

Microgreens and Other Food Trends

The Rise of Microgreens

Microgreens are the unlikely celebrities of the food world. Who would have thought that tiny, baby plants could steal the spotlight from their fully grown counterparts? Yet, here they are, gracing Instagram feeds, high-end restaurant plates, and the occasional overambitious home cook's kitchen counter. It's as if these tiny sprouts have been crowned royalty, and we're all scrambling to figure out why.

At first glance, microgreens seem unassuming. They're just baby versions of regular vegetables and herbs, harvested when they're barely a few inches tall. But somewhere along the way, they went from being ignored to being exalted as the next big thing in "superfoods." Maybe it's their petite size or their delicate appearance that makes them feel exclusive, almost like they belong to a secret culinary elite. Or maybe it's because they're marketed as nutrient powerhouses, promising to deliver everything from glowing skin to superhuman energy in just a handful of sprouts. Who wouldn't want to sprinkle a little magic on their dal or salad?

But let's not forget the real genius behind their rise: clever marketing. Somewhere, someone decided to call them "microgreens" instead of "baby plants," and the rest is history. It's the kind of branding wizardry that can turn a ₹10 ka dhaniya (₹10 bunch of coriander) into a ₹500 garnish. Once you slap a fancy label on them, they're no longer just tiny leaves—they're an experience. A sprinkle of microgreens on your pasta is a way of saying, "I'm sophisticated, I know my food, and yes, I will post this on Instagram."

Of course, microgreens have also found their way into every upscale dining establishment. Gone are the days when a simple coriander garnish sufficed. Now, it's all about a "generous dusting of microgreens," which is fancy talk for "we put three sprigs of basil's baby cousin on your dish and charged you ₹200 extra for it." It's the culinary equivalent of paying a premium for designer ripped jeans—they're smaller, less functional, and somehow more expensive.

The irony is that microgreens aren't some rare, exotic discovery—they're something our grandmothers would have probably scoffed at. "Why are you paying so much for sprouts? Just grow them in a bowl of water," your dadi (grandmother) might say. And she'd be right. Because at the end of the day, microgreens are essentially what happens when you don't let your methi (fenugreek) grow up.

Hype vs Reality

The idea of growing microgreens at home sounds delightful—until you try it. The internet makes it look so simple: sprinkle some seeds, keep them moist, and voilà, you'll have an edible garden in a week. But for most of us, the reality is more like: sprinkle seeds, forget to water them, and end up with a sad, shrivelled mess that vaguely resembles grass clippings.

The practicality of microgreens begins to unravel the moment you realize they're essentially the picky divas of the plant world. They demand just the right amount of water—not too much, not too little. They need a perfect balance of sunlight and shade, as if they're auditioning for a lead role in a Bollywood drama. And don't even get me started on the temperature. One wrong move, and you're left with a soggy patch of lifeless sprouts that couldn't sustain a mosquito, let alone a human.

Take my own attempt at growing microgreens, for example. Armed with enthusiasm and a packet of seeds, I decided to transform my kitchen windowsill into a farm-to-table haven. Day 1: planted seeds, feeling smug. Day 3: tiny sprouts appeared, and I was already imagining Instagram-worthy salads. Day 7: the microgreens looked more like "micro-yellows." By Day 10, I was forced to admit defeat and ordered pizza instead. It turns out, growing microgreens is less "fun hobby" and more "full-time job."

The absurdity doesn't stop there. Let's say you manage to grow a batch of microgreens successfully—congratulations! Now what? After all that effort, you're left with a teaspoon of garnish, barely enough to cover one slice of toast. The payoff feels disproportionate to the work you've put in. It's like spending hours cooking a gourmet meal, only to find out the recipe serves half a person.

And yet, despite all this, the hype around microgreens refuses to die down. Maybe it's because they've become a status symbol—a way to show that you're not just eating food, you're curating an experience. Having microgreens on your plate says, "I care about nutrition, aesthetics, and being ahead of the trend curve." Never mind that your plate looks like it's been sprinkled with the aftermath of lawn mowing.

The truth is, microgreens are less about practicality and more about presentation. They're the culinary equivalent of those expensive, minimalist gadgets that promise to "simplify your life" but mostly just sit on your countertop collecting dust. Sure, they look good in theory, but in real life, they're high-maintenance, finicky, and ultimately more trouble than they're worth.

When Greens Go Gourmet

Microgreens have officially made their way into the realm of haute cuisine, and boy, do they know how to milk it. Once confined to niche food circles and farmer's markets, these tiny greens are now the undisputed stars of fine dining. But let's be honest: they're less about sustenance and more about signalling sophistication. Sprinkle a few microgreens on a plate, and suddenly it's no longer just "dal with a side of sabzi (vegetable curry)"—it's "artisanal lentil stew with a curated herbaceous garnish."

Take any upscale restaurant menu today, and you'll notice microgreens listed as though they're a VIP ingredient. Dishes aren't simply "served" with microgreens; they're "elevated" by them. A plate of spaghetti is transformed into "handcrafted linguine adorned with pea tendrils." A simple tomato soup? Now it's "heirloom tomato bisque, finished with a delicate dusting of basil microgreens." It's the same dish you'd make at home, but 300% more expensive because a chef decided to scatter baby plants on top.

The pretentiousness doesn't stop there. Microgreens have also become a favourite of chefs competing on reality cooking shows. You'll hear them saying things like, "The radish microgreens add a peppery dimension to balance the dish's umami profile." Meanwhile, the judges nod solemnly, as if these greens are unlocking the secrets of the universe. The irony is that most of us couldn't tell the difference between arugula and rocket greens, let alone the subtleties of "peppery dimension."

And it's not just in restaurants—microgreens have wormed their way into home dining, too. Enter the "gourmet home chef," a species that thrives on Instagram and finds joy in plating food that looks like a masterpiece but probably tastes like everyone else's aloo paratha (stuffed flatbread). Their captions often read, "Just whipped up a quick breakfast: avocado toast with kale microgreens, Himalayan pink salt, and a dash of truffle oil." Quick breakfast?

That's at least 20 minutes of plating and an existential debate over which angle best showcases the microgreens.

The funny thing is microgreens weren't always so pretentious. Traditionally, they were a practical, no-frills way to get some nutrition during off-seasons. Farmers used to grow them as an efficient way to make the most of small spaces. But somewhere along the way, they shed their humble roots and became symbols of luxury. What was once a frugal choice has been rebranded into a premium experience.

Yet, for all their gourmet appeal, the role of microgreens is ultimately decorative. They're not here to fill you up or nourish you deeply—they're here to make your food look like it belongs on the cover of a magazine. And hey, maybe that's okay. Sometimes, food isn't just about eating; it's about the story it tells. And if microgreens help you tell a story of sophistication, trendiness, and a little bit of humour, then maybe they're worth the hype—just don't expect them to replace your sabzi (vegetables) anytime soon.

Mango Madness and the Joy of Seasons

Mango Season: A National Obsession

In India, mango season isn't just a time of year—it's a nationwide celebration that feels almost sacred. The moment the first mangoes of the season hit the markets, the air is charged with excitement. People rush to buy their favourite varieties, homes are stocked with crates of golden fruit, and every conversation revolves around mangoes. "Have you tasted the Alphonsos this year?" or "Langda or Dasheri—which one's better?" become questions of critical importance.

Each region proudly champions its mangoes. Maharashtra's Alphonso, known for its creamy texture and luxurious sweetness, often leads the pack, but Uttar Pradesh's Dasheri, Bengal's Himsagar, and Gujarat's Kesar are no less celebrated. Mango loyalty runs deep, and debates over which variety deserves the crown can rival cricket rivalries. In truth, there's no wrong answer—every mango brings its own charm.

Mango season is as much about nostalgia as it is about indulgence. Families come together, sitting cross-legged on the floor with mangoes piled high, peeling and eating them with a sense of ceremony. For children, it's a time of sticky hands, juice-smeared faces, and laughter. Elders reminisce about their childhood summers, recounting stories of climbing mango trees or sneaking bites from the crates meant for pickling. The aroma of ripe mangoes fills every home, a sweet signal that summer has truly arrived.

Beyond eating mangoes fresh, kitchens transform into hubs of mango creativity. Aamras (sweet mango pulp) served with puris becomes a staple meal, tangy mango pickles are prepared in bulk, and refreshing mango lassis help beat the heat. Each recipe feels like an ode to the fruit, celebrating its versatility and irresistible flavour. But no matter how many culinary forms mangoes take, there's a primal joy in biting straight into the fruit, letting the juice drip freely, and savouring its unadulterated sweetness.

And then there are the mango-eating competitions—the ultimate testament to India's love affair with mangoes. I still remember the day I competed in (and proudly won) one such contest. The rules were deceptively simple: eat as many mangoes as you can in ten minutes. The reality, however, was pure chaos. The whistle blew, and it was mayhem. Juice splattered everywhere, mango skins were tossed aside like battlefield debris, and competitors turned into sticky, determined warriors.

Some participants attempted a delicate peel-first approach, but I knew better. My strategy was simple: dive in and devour. I squeezed the fruit straight into my mouth, tossing the skins aside with practiced efficiency. By the time the timer ran out, I was crowned champion, my face and hands smeared with pulp and my heart full of mango glory. Winning wasn't just about the bragging rights—it was about celebrating the pure, unrestrained joy of mango season.

These competitions aren't just about eating—they're about connection. They turn mangoes into a shared experience, bringing people together to laugh, cheer, and indulge in friendly rivalry. Kids watch wide-eyed, cheering on their favourite contestant, while elders in the crowd shout encouragement and offer unsolicited strategies ("Eat the Alphonsos first—they're softer!"). It's messy, chaotic, and undeniably fun.

But mango overindulgence isn't limited to competitions. The entire season is a time of joyful excess. Diets are thrown out the window, and the mantra becomes, "Just one more." Midnight trips to the kitchen for a mango snack are common, and no family gathering is complete without a centrepiece of perfectly ripened mangoes. Crates disappear faster than you'd expect, and no one complains about eating mangoes every day. If anything, the only complaint is when the season ends too soon.

Shopping for mangoes is an event. The local sabziwala (vegetable vendor) transforms into a mango expert, offering advice on how to pick the best fruit. "Press near the stem, madam—it should be soft," they'll say, or, "This one's for today, but that one needs two more days to ripen." Markets are filled with the heady aroma of ripe mangoes, and the act of choosing them becomes a sensory experience. Smelling, pressing, and examining each fruit feels like a sacred ritual, a small but meaningful part of the season's joy.

Mango season isn't just about the fruit—it's about the memories it creates. It's about the sticky hands of childhood, the laughter of family gatherings, and the satisfaction of savouring something that feels like a gift from nature. For those few months, life feels sweeter, simpler, and more connected. And when the season inevitably ends, the wait for next year begins, filled with anticipation and the promise of more mango-filled moments.

The Joy of Overindulgence

When it comes to seasonal food in India, restraint is often the first casualty. There's something about the arrival of a favourite fruit or vegetable that flips a switch in the brain, urging you to abandon moderation. From competitive eating to bizarre culinary experiments, seasonal overindulgence is practically a national pastime.

Take mangoes, for instance. Every household has someone who turns into a mango-hoarding maniac during summer. This person meticulously organizes mangoes by ripeness in the fridge, guarding them like state secrets. They'll ration the best Alphonsos to themselves, leaving the rest of the family with "practice mangoes" that are either overripe or underripe. It's a role that creates family legends. "Remember that summer when Dad hid the mangoes under the onions?"

And then there's the strange hierarchy of seasonal dishes. Winter gajar ka halwa is revered to the point where people have absurd expectations about it. I've seen families taste-test halwa with the scrutiny of a Michelin inspector, debating if the carrots were grated fine enough or whether the sugar-to-ghee ratio was perfect. In contrast, peas—while loved—are treated like snacks to be stolen. The same uncle who demands precision in his halwa will be caught red-handed eating raw peas straight from the pod, claiming they were "testing for sweetness."

Of course, overindulgence isn't limited to eating. It extends to the ritual of buying seasonal produce. The act of shopping becomes an Olympic sport. During guava season, my mother used to sniff every guava in the pile, testing their ripeness. It wasn't just shopping; it was performance art. Vendors, likely amused, would watch patiently until she settled on "the one," treating the guava like it held the secrets of the universe.

Mango-buying, though, takes the cake. Have you ever seen a mango fanatic negotiate at a roadside stall? It's a dance of flattery and threats. "Bhaiya (brother), these don't look like Ratnagiri Alphonsos! Are you trying to pass them off as Kesar?" The vendor, undeterred, responds with a proud explanation of his mango's pedigree. This goes on until a deal is struck—or until another customer distracts the vendor long enough for you to sneakily inspect the mangoes again.

Seasonal indulgence also leads to highly questionable food experiments. Remember the mango-only meal phase? Some households decide that a single fruit must dominate every course. Mango milkshakes for breakfast, aamras for lunch, mango salads for snacks, and mango kulfi for dessert. While charming on the first day, by the second, the family starts inventing excuses. "Should we try watermelon for a change?"

But it's not just mangoes that inspire culinary creativity. My cousin once decided to use leftover sarson ka saag as pizza topping, claiming it was "fusion cuisine." To this day, our family refers to it as "Punjabi disaster pizza." Meanwhile, monsoon tamarind makes even the most disciplined eater forget their limits. Have you ever tried eating tamarind while simultaneously daring yourself to handle its sourness? One bite leads to another, and before you know it, you're surrounded by sticky tamarind seeds and wondering why your jaw hurts.

The beauty of overindulgence lies in its communal nature. Seasonal food isn't something you savour alone; it's a collective experience. Families bond over shared gluttony, swapping stories, competing for the best slice, and arguing over who ate the last portion. Even the mess becomes a memory—peels piling up, sticky hands being wiped on anything nearby, and mango stains appearing mysteriously on white shirts.

In India, overindulgence isn't just about excess—it's about savouring abundance. It's the joy of letting yourself go, of celebrating nature's fleeting gifts with enthusiasm. Whether it's guavas, corn, or the inevitable mango feast, we dive in with laughter, sticky hands, and absolutely no regrets.

Seasons Beyond Mangoes

While mango season reigns supreme, India's other seasonal produce offers a treasure trove of delights. Every season brings its own heroes—fruits and vegetables that capture the essence of their time, offering not just nourishment but also nostalgia and joy.

Take winter, for instance. When the chill sets in, the streets come alive with guava vendors pushing carts piled high with green, fragrant fruit. There's a specific art to eating a guava: slicing it open, sprinkling it with salt and chili powder, and taking that first tangy, crunchy bite. For many, it's a taste that transports them straight back to childhood. Memories of sneaking guavas from the neighbour's tree or buying them fresh after school come rushing back with every mouthful. And then there's the debate: do you eat the seeds or spit them out? The answer, of course, is personal—and often fiercely defended.

Monsoons, on the other hand, bring with them the smoky aroma of bhutta (roasted corn). Street vendors set up shop wherever the rains fall, fanning coal fires and roasting corn to perfection. The smell of charred kernels mingling with the earthy scent of wet soil is enough to draw anyone in. Eating bhutta is a ritual in itself: rubbing the cob with lime, sprinkling it with salt and chili, and biting into it while dodging the occasional drizzle. It's a snack that's as much about the experience as it is about the flavour—a rainy-day indulgence that feels like a warm hug from the season.

Spring is all about tender green peas, or matar, which seem to make their way into every dish imaginable. From aloo matar (potato and pea curry) to fresh peas stuffed into parathas, their short season ensures they're celebrated with enthusiasm. The act of shelling peas—popping them out of their pods, one by one—is oddly therapeutic, often done in the company of family members sharing stories and laughter. For kids, sneaking a handful of raw peas to munch on is part of the fun. It's these little moments that make seasonal eating more than just about food—it's about connection.

And then there's winter's crowning glory: carrots. Not just any carrots, but the deep red ones that signal the arrival of gajar ka halwa (carrot pudding). This rich, indulgent dessert is a labour of love, made by slow-cooking grated carrots with milk, sugar, and ghee, and garnishing it with nuts and raisins. Every bite is a reminder of winter gatherings, cozy evenings, and the comfort of tradition. For many, gajar ka halwa isn't just a treat—it's a memory on a plate.

Each season's produce comes with its own stories and rituals, and eating with the seasons is about more than just flavour. It's a way of embracing nature's rhythms, celebrating the fleeting joys of seasonal fruits and vegetables, and finding beauty in what's available right now. In a world where supermarkets offer everything all the time, choosing to eat seasonally feels like a small rebellion against instant gratification. It's about patience and anticipation—the kind that makes the first mango of summer or the first guava of winter taste even sweeter.

Seasonal eating also offers practical benefits. Fruits and vegetables grown in their natural season are at their peak in terms of flavour and nutrition. A winter guava, for instance, is bursting with vitamin C, helping you fend off seasonal colds, while summer cucumbers are hydrating and cooling, perfect for combating the heat. Nature, it seems, knows exactly what we need at any given time. By eating seasonally, we're aligning with this wisdom, letting the earth guide our diets in a way that's as nourishing as it is satisfying.

To better appreciate the rhythm of Indian seasons, here's a quick guide to what nature offers throughout the year:

Season	Fruits	Vegetables
Summer	Mango, Jamun (Indian blackberry), Watermelon, Lychee, Papaya, Muskmelon	Cucumber, Pumpkin, Ridge Gourd, Bitter Gourd
Monsoon	Jamun, Pear, Pomegranate, Plum	Corn (Bhutta), Drumstick, Spinach, Amaranth
Winter	Guava, Orange, Apple, Custard Apple, Amla (Indian Gooseberry)	Carrot, Peas, Cauliflower, Radish, Mustard Greens
Spring	Strawberry, Grapefruit, Pineapple	Broad Beans, Green Peas, Spring Onion, Fenugreek (Methi)

Seasonal eating also helps reduce environmental impact. Seasonal, local produce has a much smaller carbon footprint than off-season imports. That mango in December or strawberry in June has likely travelled thousands of kilometres, leaving behind a trail of emissions. In contrast, a winter guava or monsoon corn from a local farm is not only fresher but also kinder to the planet. By eating with the seasons, we support local farmers, reduce transportation and storage costs, and promote a food system that's more sustainable and connected to the land.

But beyond the environmental and health benefits, seasonal eating is about savouring life's small joys. It's about looking forward to the first bhutta of the monsoon, the tangy burst of raw tamarind in summer, or the warmth of sarson ka saag (mustard greens) in winter. Each fruit and vegetable has its moment in the sun, and when it's gone, it leaves behind a craving that makes its return all the more special.

Imagine biting into a crisp winter apple, its sweetness and tartness perfectly balanced, or relishing the juicy tang of jamuns in the early monsoon. These moments remind us of the simple pleasures that food can bring, especially when it's enjoyed in its natural time. Seasonal eating teaches us to slow down, appreciate the cycles of nature, and find contentment in what's in front of us.

And it's not just about the individual fruits and vegetables—it's about the traditions they inspire. A summer without mango feasts, a monsoon without bhutta, or a winter without gajar ka halwa feels incomplete. These foods aren't just nourishment—they're part of our identity, woven into the fabric of who we are and where we come from. By eating seasonally, we're keeping these traditions alive, passing them down to future generations with every bite.

Local Markets: Real Freshness, Real Chaos

There's a unique charm to shopping at a local sabzi mandi (vegetable market)—a charm that no sterile supermarket aisle can replicate. It's chaos, yes, but it's the kind of chaos that energizes you, immerses you in a sensory experience, and connects you to the stories behind your food. The mandi is more than a place to shop; it's a vibrant community hub, an open-air theatre where every vendor, customer, and fruit pile plays a role.

The first thing that hits you as you enter a mandi is the noise. Vendors calling out their prices in rhythmic chants, haggling customers making counteroffers, and the occasional scuffle over whose turn it is to buy coriander—all of it blends into a symphony of daily life. It's not just noise; it's music, the heartbeat of a neighbourhood starting its day. And if you listen closely, you'll notice that every vendor has their own unique style. There's the enthusiastic tomato seller shouting, "Ek kilo ke saath ek adrak free, behenji (Free ginger with every kilo, madam)!" and the onion vendor with a flair for humour: "Yeh pyaaz roti khilayega, rulaayega nahi (These onions will complement your roti, not make you cry)."

Shopping at a mandi is a test of skill. First, there's the art of haggling. If you're too timid, you'll end up paying more than your neighbour for the same kilo of potatoes. But if you're too aggressive, you risk losing the vendor's goodwill and that bonus bunch of dhaniya (coriander). My grandmother was a master negotiator. She had a way of feigning disinterest while subtly nudging the vendor toward a better deal. "Is this the best you can do?" she'd ask with mock disappointment, holding up a tomato as if it had personally offended her. Often, she'd walk away triumphant, a bunch of free curry leaves tucked into her bag as proof of her victory.

Then there's the act of choosing the freshest produce—a ritual that borders on performance art. Watching seasoned shoppers at a mandi is like attending a masterclass in produce evaluation. They sniff guavas, press cucumbers, and shake bunches of spinach to see if they're sturdy enough. The untrained eye might think they're overanalysing, but they know exactly what they're looking for. My mother once rejected an entire pile of apples because "the stems looked too dry," a detail so specific that even the vendor was impressed.

The mandi isn't just about buying vegetables; it's about building relationships. Regular customers and vendors share a bond built on trust, banter, and familiarity. "Behenji, kal toh aapne bina baat kiye chhod diya! Aaj le jao (Madam, yesterday you ignored me without a word! Take something today)," a vendor might call out, half-jokingly. These relationships often come with perks: a better price, the freshest produce, or an extra handful of green chilies tossed in as a gesture of goodwill.

But it's not all smooth sailing. The mandi can also be a battlefield. I once watched two women argue passionately over the last ripe papaya in a stall. Their debate over whose papaya "rights" were stronger drew such a crowd that the vendor had to intervene. His solution? He sold the papaya to a third person entirely, declaring it "neutral territory."

The sensory overload of a mandi is part of its charm. The vibrant colours of fruits and vegetables—shiny purple brinjals, vivid green spinach, and golden yellow bananas—create a visual feast. The smell is equally intoxicating: the earthy aroma of fresh coriander mingling with the sweetness of ripe guavas and the occasional whiff of fried pakoras from a nearby street stall. Every mandi visit feels like a little adventure, a reminder that shopping for food can be as enjoyable as eating it.

And then there are the characters. Every mandi has its iconic figures—the loud vendor who everyone loves, the quiet one who sells the best spinach, and the customer who somehow always manages to get a better deal than anyone else. In my local mandi, there was an old vendor we called "Tomato Baba." He'd sit cross-legged on a wooden crate, sorting his tomatoes with a precision that bordered on meditation. No one dared haggle with him because his produce was so flawless that it sold itself.

But the mandi isn't just a marketplace—it's a cultural hub. It's where neighbours meet and catch up, where recipes are exchanged, and where food becomes a conversation. "Kya banayenge aaj? Baingan bharte ke liye yeh perfect hai (What will you cook today? This is perfect for baingan bharta)," a vendor might suggest, turning a routine transaction into a moment of connection. The mandi fosters a sense of community, reminding you that food isn't just a commodity; it's a shared experience.

In the age of supermarkets and online grocery delivery, the mandi remains a bastion of authenticity. It's imperfect, chaotic, and sometimes frustrating, but it's also alive in a way that no supermarket aisle could ever replicate. Shopping at a mandi is more than a task—

it's an event, one that leaves you with not just a bag full of vegetables but also stories to tell.

For me, the mandi is a place of memories. It's where my grandmother taught me the art of picking the best mangoes, where my mother haggled her way into fame among the vendors, and where I once bought an entire basket of guavas simply because the vendor's description of them was so poetic. It's messy, it's noisy, and it's utterly irreplaceable.

Chapter 2

Non-Stick Nonsense – Why Your Cookware Might Be Plotting Against You

The Cookware Conundrum: What's Wrong with Your Pots and Pans?

Non-Stick Teflon and PFAS Coatings: The Convenience Trap

Non-stick cookware has an irresistible allure. It promises ease, efficiency, and that magical moment where a perfectly fried egg slides out of the pan without leaving even a trace behind. It's the superhero of kitchen convenience—or so the ads claim. But like every superhero, it has a dark side, one that's more chemical villain than culinary marvel. If your trusty non-stick pan could talk, it would tell you a chilling story of toxins, health risks, and dubious marketing promises.

The Illusion of Effortlessness

Non-stick pans first entered the scene as a miracle for the modern cook. They eliminated the need for excessive oil, made cleaning a breeze, and spared us the indignity of scraping burnt remnants off our cookware. But this so-called magic comes with conditions no one talks about.

Don't heat it too high. Don't use metal utensils. Don't put it in the dishwasher. Oh, and if it scratches? Well, it's basically a chemical cocktail waiting to be stirred into your morning omelette.

At the heart of this convenience is Teflon, a material made of PTFE (polytetrafluoroethylene). While PTFE gives the pan its slippery surface, it also makes it fragile under the intense conditions of Indian kitchens. From deep-fried samosas to a sizzling tadka, high-heat cooking is a way of life—and this is where non-stick cookware begins to unravel, quite literally.

"Teflon Flu" and Toxic Fumes

Let's talk temperatures. Teflon starts to break down at around 260°C (500°F), and by the time you crank up the flame to make a perfect aloo paratha, your pan might already be emitting fumes. These fumes contain toxic particles that can cause a condition charmingly nicknamed "Teflon flu," or polymer fume fever.

Symptoms include headaches, fever, and nausea—not exactly what you'd want to serve alongside your dinner. The real kicker? These fumes are lethal to pet birds, whose sensitive respiratory systems can't handle the chemicals. If it can kill a parrot, maybe it's time to rethink that non-stick dosa tawa.

PTFE and PFAS: The Forever Chemicals

The story doesn't end with fumes. Non-stick cookware also contains PFAS (per- and polyfluoroalkyl substances), a class of chemicals that gives the surface its water and oil-repellent properties. These substances are often called "forever chemicals" because they don't break down in the environment or in our bodies. Instead, they accumulate over time, with potential effects on health that range from the mildly concerning to the downright terrifying.

Studies have linked PFAS exposure to:

- **Cancer**: Increased risks of liver, kidney, and testicular cancers.

- **Hormonal Disruption**: Interference with reproductive and thyroid hormones, which can lead to fertility issues and metabolic disorders.

- **Immune System Damage**: PFAS exposure has been shown to weaken immunity, reducing vaccine effectiveness and increasing susceptibility to infections.

These chemicals have been found in water, air, and even human blood, and while cookware may only contribute a small fraction of the exposure, every scratch on your pan means more leaching into your food—and eventually, your body.

Microplastics: The Invisible Guests

As non-stick pans age, they inevitably start to flake. The once-smooth surface becomes pitted and scratched, releasing tiny pieces of PTFE into your food. These microplastics are nearly impossible for the body to process and are suspected to contribute to a host of long-term health issues, including metabolic disruption, chronic inflammation, and oxidative stress.

Imagine preparing a comforting bowl of dal only to realize you've accidentally seasoned it with invisible plastic particles. Not quite the wholesome meal you were going for, is it?

The Non-Stick Hustle

It's not just the chemicals that are the problem; it's the marketing. Brands present non-stick cookware as an essential kitchen item, highlighting ease of use and "healthier" cooking. After all, who wouldn't want to use less oil? But what they don't tell you is that non-stick coatings are anything but durable. Even with gentle use, they degrade within a few years, leaving behind scratched surfaces that are both unsafe and ineffective.

This means you're constantly replacing them, funnelling more money into cookware that isn't built to last. Over time, the cost of non-stick pans can far exceed that of a single high-quality enamel-coated cast iron skillet or titanium pan, both of which offer genuine durability and safety.

Aluminium: Budget-Friendly but Brain-Unfriendly

Aluminium is the underdog of Indian kitchens. Affordable, lightweight, and great at conducting heat, it's the cookware equivalent of your trusty autorickshaw—reliable but with a questionable track record when it comes to long-term performance. From pressure cookers to kadhais (deep cooking pots), aluminium is everywhere. But while it wins points for accessibility, what it's doing to your health is a story no one likes to talk about.

The Metal That Loves to Share

Aluminium is reactive, which means it's not content to just sit there and cook your food. No, it wants to participate. When exposed to high heat or acidic foods like tomatoes, tamarind, or yogurt, aluminium leaches into your meal. And unlike a generous pinch of garam masala, this is an ingredient you don't want.

Studies have shown that small amounts of aluminium can transfer to food during cooking, particularly when preparing acidic or salty dishes. The leaching increases with wear and tear, so the older your aluminium cookware, the more it shares. And let's face it—most of us aren't replacing that aluminium kadhai our mother-in-law gifted us 15 years ago.

The Brain-Busting Backstory

What's the big deal about a little aluminium in your food? Well, here's the kicker: aluminium exposure has been linked to a range of health issues, particularly neurotoxicity. Some studies suggest a connection between chronic aluminium exposure and cognitive decline, including Alzheimer's disease. While the research is still evolving, the evidence is concerning enough to warrant attention—especially for those of us cooking multiple meals a day in aluminium pots.

Think of it this way: every time you make a tangy tomato curry or a yogurt-based marinade in an aluminium vessel, you're not just preparing dinner—you're potentially seasoning your neurons with trace metals. Over time, these metals can accumulate in the brain, disrupting normal functions and increasing oxidative stress.

Not Just the Brain—Your Kidneys are Listening

If aluminium's assault on your brain isn't enough to give you pause, consider its impact on your kidneys. The kidneys are your body's filtration system, tasked with removing excess metals and toxins. But when you're constantly exposed to aluminium through cookware, water, and even food packaging, your kidneys can become overwhelmed.

For people with compromised kidney function, this can be particularly dangerous. Studies have shown that individuals with kidney issues absorb aluminium more readily, increasing the risk of further damage. Even in healthy individuals, prolonged exposure can strain this vital organ, leading to long-term health concerns.

Bones of Contention

One lesser-known consequence of aluminium exposure is its effect on bone health. Aluminium interferes with calcium metabolism, which is essential for maintaining strong bones. Over time, this can lead to conditions like osteomalacia (softening of the bones) or increased susceptibility to fractures. While this may not seem immediately relevant to your cooking habits, think about the cumulative effect of years of aluminium exposure, especially in diets already lacking in calcium.

The Acid Test: Why Indian Cooking Makes It Worse

Indian cuisine is a perfect storm for aluminium leaching. Many of our beloved dishes—whether it's a tamarind-laden sambhar, a tomato-heavy masala, or a yogurt-based raita—are highly acidic. Combine that with high-heat cooking techniques like frying and simmering, and you've got the ideal conditions for aluminium to make its way into your meals.

Take the humble pressure cooker, a staple in most Indian households. Pressure cooking involves both high heat and prolonged cooking times, two factors that accelerate metal leaching. If your pressure cooker is made of uncoated aluminium, it's essentially a metal-dispensing machine disguised as a time-saver.

The Shiny Myth of Anodized Aluminium

To counteract the downsides of plain aluminium, manufacturers have introduced anodized aluminium cookware. This type of cookware has undergone an electrochemical process that creates a protective oxide layer, making it more resistant to leaching. Sounds great, right? Not so fast.

While anodized aluminium is certainly safer than its uncoated counterpart, it's not foolproof. The protective layer can wear down over time, especially if the cookware is scratched or subjected to harsh cleaning. Once that happens, you're back to square one with metal leaching. So while anodized aluminium is a step up, it's still not the long-term solution many people hope it to be.

Why Cheap Isn't Always Cheerful

Aluminium's biggest selling point is its price. It's one of the most affordable cookware materials on the market, making it a go-to choice for budget-conscious households. But what often gets overlooked is the hidden cost of using aluminium over the long term.

Consider this: replacing your health with a slightly cheaper cooking pot isn't exactly a win-win scenario. While aluminium may save you a few rupees upfront, the potential costs to your health—from medical bills to reduced quality of life—can far outweigh the savings.

Stainless Steel: The Sneaky Culprit

Stainless steel. The name itself exudes reliability, doesn't it? It's shiny, durable, and practically synonymous with the modern Indian kitchen. From pressure cookers to spice boxes, stainless steel seems like the gold standard of cookware. But while it's often touted as non-reactive and safe, stainless steel has a few secrets tucked beneath that glossy surface.

The Shine That Blinds Us

Stainless steel owes its shiny, rust-resistant surface to a combination of metals—primarily iron, chromium, and nickel. It's this alloying that makes it "stainless," a material that resists corrosion and holds up to the rigors of daily cooking. But here's the twist: those same metals can leach into your food under the right conditions. Yes, even stainless steel isn't completely innocent.

The extent of leaching depends on the grade of stainless steel, the type of food being cooked, and the heat level. While it's true that stainless steel is far safer than aluminium or non-stick coatings, its Achilles' heel is acidic cooking—something Indian cuisine specializes in.

Nickel: A Shiny Villain

Nickel, one of the key components of stainless steel, is what gives the material its shiny finish and rust resistance. But nickel is also a known allergen, and around 5-10% of people are sensitive to it. If you're part of this group, even trace amounts of nickel can trigger reactions ranging from skin rashes to respiratory issues.

And nickel sensitivity isn't the only concern. Chronic exposure to nickel through cooking can have long-term health effects, including an increased risk of cancer in high-exposure environments. While cooking a single batch of tamarind-based rasam in a stainless-steel pot won't turn you into a toxic soup, the cumulative exposure from daily use can add up over time.

Chromium: The Double-Edged Sword

Chromium is another key player in stainless steel, contributing to its durability and corrosion resistance. In small amounts, chromium is beneficial for health, playing a role in glucose metabolism and insulin regulation. But, as with nickel, too much of a good thing can become a problem.

When you cook acidic foods like tomatoes, lemon juice, or yogurt in stainless steel, the chromium in the material can leach into your food. While the leached amounts are generally small, they can build up over time, particularly if you're using lower-quality stainless steel or cooking acidic dishes frequently.

Acidity: Stainless Steel's Kryptonite

Let's talk about acidic foods. They're a cornerstone of Indian cooking, whether it's tangy tomato curries, yogurt-based marinades, or lemon-laced dals. Unfortunately, these acidic ingredients are stainless steels kryptonite. The acidity reacts with the metals in the cookware, increasing the likelihood of nickel and chromium leaching into your meals.

For most people, these trace amounts won't pose an immediate health risk. But if you're someone who uses stainless steel cookware for almost everything—boiling tamarind pulp, simmering tomato-based gravies, or even making pickles—the exposure can add up over time.

Not All Stainless Steel is Created Equal

The good news? Stainless steel comes in different grades, and some are safer than others. These grades are usually labelled with numbers like 18/10, 18/8, or 18/0, which indicate the proportions of chromium and nickel in the alloy.

- **18/10 Stainless Steel**: Contains 18% chromium and 10% nickel. This is the most common grade and is highly resistant to rust and corrosion. However, it has the highest nickel content, making it less suitable for people with nickel sensitivity.

- **18/8 Stainless Steel**: Contains 18% chromium and 8% nickel. Slightly lower in nickel than 18/10, but still not ideal for those with allergies.

- **18/0 Stainless Steel**: Contains 18% chromium and zero nickel. This is the best choice for people with nickel sensitivity, though it's slightly less resistant to rust.

If you're unsure about the grade of your stainless-steel cookware, it's worth checking with the manufacturer or opting for a brand that clearly labels its products.

Scratched Steel: A Leaching Nightmare

Stainless steel is generally safe when it's in good condition. But scratches, dents, and wear-and-tear can compromise its protective surface, increasing the likelihood of leaching. Unfortunately, most of us don't treat our cookware with kid gloves—stainless steel pans often face the brunt of metal spatulas, harsh scrubbers, and high-heat cooking.

Once the surface is compromised, the leaching of metals like nickel and chromium becomes significantly more pronounced. This is why it's essential to replace old or damaged stainless-steel cookware and avoid using abrasive cleaning tools that can scratch the surface.

Indian Kitchens and Stainless Steel: A Complicated Love Affair

Stainless steel holds a special place in Indian kitchens. It's almost a rite of passage to inherit a set of stainless-steel utensils from your parents or grandparents. But our love for stainless steel sometimes blinds us to its limitations.

Take pressure cookers, for example. While stainless steel cookers are less reactive than aluminium ones, they're not entirely immune to leaching—especially when used to cook tangy dals or tamarind-laden sambhars under high pressure. The combination of acidity, high heat, and prolonged cooking time creates a perfect storm for metal leaching.

How to Use Stainless Steel Safely

Stainless steel isn't the villain of this cookware saga—it's more like the frenemy who's mostly dependable but occasionally lets you down. Here's how to get the most out of your stainless-steel cookware while minimizing its quirks:

1. **Avoid Prolonged Cooking of Acidic Foods**: Use stainless steel for steaming, boiling, or frying rather than for acidic recipes. For tamarind curries or tomato-based gravies, opt for non-reactive options like enamel-coated cast iron or glass cookware.

2. **Choose the Right Grade**: If nickel sensitivity is a concern, look for 18/0 stainless steel cookware. It's slightly less shiny but much safer for those with allergies.

3. **Replace Damaged Cookware**: Don't hold onto scratched, dented, or heavily worn stainless steel pots and pans. Damaged surfaces are more prone to leaching and should be replaced promptly.

4. **Cook at Medium Heat**: High heat increases the risk of leaching, so stick to medium or low heat when using stainless steel cookware.

Ceramic-Coated Cookware: The "Healthy" Myth

Ceramic-coated cookware enters the kitchen as a saviour, flaunting its glossy surface and a promise of toxin-free cooking. It looks so innocent, marketed as an upgrade from traditional non-stick, offering an eco-friendly alternative free from chemicals like PFAS or PTFE. For the health-conscious home cook, it seems like the answer to everything. But behind its colourful facade lies a story that's less about health and more about compromise.

The appeal is hard to resist. A smooth, non-stick surface derived from silica, a promise of no toxic fumes even under high heat, and a product that feels as guilt-free as it is photogenic. Yet, like a glittering mirage in the desert, ceramic cookware is not all it's cracked up to be. Beneath that polished exterior lurks the risk of nanoparticles, fragile coatings, and even heavy metals sneaking into your food.

Ceramic-coated cookware isn't invincible. Over time, with repeated use and exposure to high heat, its once-pristine surface begins to degrade. This degradation can release tiny silicon-based nanoparticles into your food—particles so small they're invisible to the eye but persistent in their impact. Research into these particles is still emerging, but early findings suggest they can lead to oxidative stress and inflammation, a quiet disruption within the body. It's as if the very pan you trusted to keep things clean is adding an unwelcome seasoning of its own.

The danger doesn't stop there. Lower-quality ceramic cookware can hide a more insidious secret. Some manufacturers, in their quest to achieve vibrant colours or durable finishes, use heavy metals like lead or cadmium in their ceramic glazes. When these pans are scratched or subjected to high heat, the metals can leach into your food. Even trace amounts of lead are a serious concern, particularly for children, with effects ranging from developmental issues to long-term cognitive damage. Cadmium, meanwhile, has its own toxic repertoire, affecting kidneys and bones over time.

If the health risks weren't enough, ceramic-coated cookware also struggles with durability. Its non-stick coating fades faster than a fleeting trend. One encounter with a metal spatula or an overly aggressive cleaning session can scratch the surface, exposing the material underneath and rendering the pan unsafe. Even if you're careful, high-heat cooking—so essential in Indian kitchens—causes the coating to crack or degrade. What was once a joy to cook with becomes a stubborn liability, sticking to food and releasing particles with every use.

Despite the marketing hype, ceramic-coated cookware struggles to live up to its promises. Its non-stick capabilities are short-lived, and its safety depends heavily on how it's used and maintained. Gentle, low-heat cooking might prolong its life, but for everyday use, it's simply not built to withstand the demands of a bustling kitchen. The risks, both visible and invisible, make it a choice worth rethinking, especially when there are sturdier, safer alternatives that offer both reliability and peace of mind.

Brass and Copper: Nostalgia vs. Reality

Brass and copper cookware often evoke warm memories of family kitchens—gleaming vessels, lovingly passed down through generations, simmering curries and bubbling milk. These metals have a heritage as rich as the Flavors they promise to enhance. Yet, as much as we romanticize them, their reality in modern kitchens comes with caveats that are hard to ignore.

Brass, an alloy of copper and zinc, is celebrated for its ability to retain heat and cook food evenly. It keeps your dal piping hot long after it's left the stove, and its golden sheen makes it an heirloom-worthy centrepiece. Copper, on the other hand, is a chef's favourite for its rapid heat conduction, perfect for delicate tasks like making sugar syrups or tempering spices. However, both metals have a knack for interacting with food in ways you wouldn't welcome.

The issue lies in their reactivity. Both brass and copper are prone to leaching metals into your food, especially when exposed to acidic ingredients like tomatoes, tamarind, or yogurt. Copper, while essential in trace amounts for health, turns toxic when ingested in excess, causing nausea, gastrointestinal distress, and in severe cases, liver damage. Zinc from brass has a similar story—it's necessary for immunity and enzyme function but not when it turns your meal into a health experiment.

Older brass cookware often comes with an even darker secret: lead. Traditional methods of crafting brass sometimes included small amounts of lead to increase durability. This lead, when leached into food, is a neurotoxin that can cause cognitive impairment, kidney damage, and developmental issues, particularly in children. Cooking your grandmother's rasam recipe in that antique brass handi might come with a side of uninvited toxicity.

Back in the day, these risks were mitigated through the practice of kalai, a tin-lining process that coated brass and copper cookware to prevent metal leaching. Kalai, however, is a fading tradition.

Few artisans offer this service anymore, and even fewer households know how to maintain the coating. Once the tin layer wears off, the cookware becomes a liability, releasing metals into every meal. The result? Nostalgia quickly turns into regret.

And then there's the maintenance. Brass and copper demand constant polishing to retain their lustre, and even then, they're quick to tarnish. Forgetting to dry them properly after washing can lead to greenish patina or black spots, adding another layer of frustration to their use. It's a delicate balancing act—too much elbow grease, and you risk damaging the tin lining; too little, and you're left with cookware that looks more like a relic than a reliable kitchen companion.

For all their charm, brass and copper are high-maintenance divas that struggle to keep up with the demands of a modern kitchen. Their risks, from metal leaching to potential lead exposure, outweigh the benefits of heat retention and aesthetic appeal. While they make for stunning serveware or occasional-use cookware, their everyday practicality pales in comparison to safer, more reliable options available today.

Safety Standards: Why Aren't They Solving This Problem?

Indian Standards vs. Global Benchmarks

In a world where cookware has evolved into an extension of our culinary dreams, the regulations governing its safety should ideally keep pace. But in India, the Bureau of Indian Standards (BIS) seems to be playing a cautious game of catch-up. While our cooking styles—think bubbling curries, tangy chutneys, and high-heat tempering—demand robust and safe cookware, the standards that ensure safety often fall short of addressing the real issues. Meanwhile, global benchmarks like those set by the FDA (Food and Drug Administration) in the United States and EC 1935:2004 in the European Union are light-years ahead in protecting consumers from cookware hazards.

The Missing Pieces in BIS Standards

The BIS framework for cookware safety covers the basics, but that's precisely where the problem lies—it's basic. It lacks the rigor to deal with the complex risks associated with modern cookware, such as toxic chemicals in non-stick coatings, heavy metal leaching from stainless steel, and the degradation of ceramic-coated pans. In a country where high-heat cooking and acidic ingredients are kitchen staples, the absence of detailed testing requirements becomes a glaring oversight.

Take PFAS and PTFE, for example—the so-called "forever chemicals" that have turned non-stick pans into a hotbed of health concerns. While FDA and EC 1935:2004 regulations impose strict limits on the presence of these substances, BIS is yet to address them comprehensively. This means that your shiny, imported non-stick pan might be leaving a toxic legacy in every dosa you flip.

Similarly, heavy metal leaching is another gray area. While BIS acknowledges the risks posed by nickel and chromium leaching from stainless steel, it doesn't enforce strict migration limits like the EC standards do. So, that acidic tomato curry simmering in your stainless-steel pot might be carrying more than just flavour—it could be an uninvited dose of chromium and nickel. For consumers, the lack of clarity makes choosing safer cookware a guessing game.

The FDA and EC 1935:2004: A Class Apart

In contrast, the FDA and EC standards operate on the principle of precaution. Their regulations aren't just reactive—they anticipate risks and enforce measures to mitigate them. Take the EC 1935:2004, for instance. It mandates extensive testing to ensure that cookware materials don't transfer harmful substances into food. The regulations even account for long-term use, ensuring that products remain safe after years of exposure to heat, acidity, and wear.

The FDA, too, excels in regulating cookware safety. It imposes strict temperature thresholds for materials like PTFE to prevent the release of toxic fumes during cooking. And unlike BIS, which relies on manufacturers' voluntary compliance in many areas, FDA standards demand mandatory labelling of materials and coatings, empowering consumers to make informed choices.

What Indian Standards Could Learn

1. **Comprehensive Testing for Chemicals and Metals**: BIS could start by mandating rigorous testing for PFAS, PTFE, and heavy metals in cookware. This would align Indian standards with global benchmarks and address the risks posed by modern cookware materials.

2. **Migration Limits for Heavy Metals**: Borrowing from the EC 1935:2004 playbook, BIS could enforce strict migration limits for substances like nickel, chromium, and lead. This would

provide a measurable safety benchmark, protecting consumers from cumulative exposure to these metals.

3. **High-Heat Testing Protocols**: Given the prevalence of high-heat cooking in Indian households, BIS standards need to include specific tests for cookware performance and safety under extreme temperatures. This would be particularly relevant for materials like stainless steel and non-stick coatings.

4. **Transparency and Labelling**: One of the most consumer-friendly aspects of FDA and EC standards is their insistence on clear labelling. If BIS were to adopt this, buyers would no longer have to play detective, hunting for clues about what their cookware is made of.

Imported Cookware: A Loophole in the System

One of the unintended consequences of weak domestic standards is the influx of subpar imported cookware. With no requirement to meet stringent BIS guidelines (because such guidelines don't exist), these products often bypass scrutiny. They look glossy, boast "modern" features, and cost half the price of premium Indian brands, but their safety credentials are dubious at best.

This is where the FDA and EC regulations shine. By applying the same standards to imported cookware, these regulatory bodies ensure that consumers don't get shortchanged on safety. BIS, on the other hand, struggles to impose similar consistency, allowing potentially harmful products to flood the market.

Why This Matters More in India

Indian kitchens are unique in their demands on cookware. The searing heat of a tawa for making rotis, the acidic tang of tamarind-based curries, the bubbling oil for frying pakoras—these are not just culinary techniques; they're stress tests for cookware. A pot or pan that might perform adequately under Western cooking styles often falters when subjected to the intensity of Indian cuisine. And yet, the standards meant to protect us fail to reflect this reality.

Without rigorous safety benchmarks, consumers are left vulnerable to health risks ranging from metal toxicity to exposure to carcinogenic fumes. The lack of awareness compounds the issue. How many of us have examined our trusty kadais and frying pans for signs of wear and tear, let alone considered what materials and coatings might be sneaking into our meals?

The Need for Reform

Strengthening BIS standards isn't just about keeping pace with the FDA and EC; it's about safeguarding the health of millions of Indian households. By incorporating global best practices, India can set a new benchmark for cookware safety, ensuring that every meal prepared in an Indian kitchen is as wholesome as it is flavourful.

This isn't just a call to action for regulators but also a wake-up call for consumers. The next time you buy cookware, look beyond the gleam and gimmicks. Ask the hard questions: What's this made of? Is it built to withstand high heat? Will it keep my food safe?

Because in a country where cooking is both an art and a tradition, the tools we use should honour that legacy—not undermine it.

Why Better Standards Matter

In India, cooking is more than a daily chore—it's an art, a tradition, and often a community event. The smoky aromas of tadka wafting through kitchens, the vibrant colours of curries, and the rhythmic flipping of dosas on sizzling tawas form the heartbeat of our culinary culture. But here's the catch: while we pour our hearts into perfecting recipes, the tools we use often go unnoticed, quietly undermining our efforts.

This lack of scrutiny wouldn't matter so much if cookware safety standards were airtight, but as we've seen, India's regulatory framework has some glaring gaps. And these gaps aren't just bureaucratic oversights; they have real, tangible effects on our health, our food, and our way of life.

The Health Impacts

The dangers of substandard cookware extend far beyond the kitchen. Each time a non-stick pan overheats or an aluminium kadhai interacts with acidic food, harmful substances leach into the dishes we lovingly prepare. These substances don't just disappear after digestion; they accumulate, contributing to long-term health problems like neurotoxicity, hormonal imbalances, and even cancer.

The effects of heavy metal exposure are particularly concerning in children, whose developing bodies are more vulnerable to toxins. Imagine the irony of preparing a nutritious tomato-based curry, packed with antioxidants, only to unknowingly add a side of leached chromium or lead. Better standards wouldn't just protect us from these risks—they'd ensure that the health benefits of our food aren't offset by hidden hazards.

Cooking Styles Demand Robust Standards

Indian cooking isn't gentle. Our cuisine thrives on extremes: high heat searing for tadka, prolonged simmering for dals, and the sharp acidity of tamarind, tomatoes, and vinegar. While Western cooking styles might not push cookware to its limits, Indian methods practically demand that it perform under pressure.

Global standards like those of the FDA and EC 1935:2004 take these variables into account, specifying how cookware should behave under heat, acidity, and repeated use. In contrast, Indian standards seem blind to these realities, treating all cookware as though it faces the same mild conditions. The result? Cookware that's ill-suited for our kitchens and regulations that leave us unprotected.

Empowering Consumers Through Transparency

Better standards wouldn't just improve the quality of cookware—they'd also empower consumers. Imagine picking up a stainless steel kadhai and seeing a label that clearly states its grade (18/10 or 18/0), its safe temperature range, and whether it's free of harmful substances like nickel. This kind of transparency would demystify cookware shopping, enabling buyers to make informed choices instead of relying on marketing gimmicks.

Bridging the Gap

For a country that takes so much pride in its food, it's time we demanded the same rigor for the tools that help create it. Better standards are about more than safety; they're about respecting the traditions, techniques, and people who make Indian cuisine what it is.

The Heroes of the Kitchen: Cookware That Solves These Issues

Enamel-Coated Cast Iron: The Stalwart of the Kitchen

When it comes to cookware that combines tradition, durability, and safety, enamel-coated cast iron takes the crown. Unlike its uncoated cousin, which requires careful seasoning and maintenance, enamel-coated cast iron offers all the benefits of cast iron—heat retention, even cooking, and non-reactivity—without any of the hassle. Its versatility makes it an indispensable tool for the Indian kitchen, handling everything from a slow-simmered dal to a high-heat stir-fry with finesse.

The Power of Heat Retention

Indian cooking thrives on intense heat and prolonged simmering, two areas where enamel-coated cast iron shines. This material heats evenly and retains that heat for a long time, ensuring every grain of rice or every lentil in your dal is cooked to perfection. Whether you're slow-cooking a rich mutton curry or preparing a biryani that requires steady, even heat, enamel-coated cast iron is a dependable ally.

Picture this: you're making rajma, a dish that demands hours of gentle simmering to meld Flavors and soften beans. A stainless-steel pot might heat unevenly, leaving you with scorched beans on the bottom and undercooked ones floating on top. Enamel-coated cast iron, with its ability to distribute heat evenly, ensures that every bite of your rajma is as delicious as the last.

A Safe Choice for Health-Conscious Cooks

One of the greatest advantages of enamel-coated cast iron is its non-reactivity. Unlike aluminium or brass, it doesn't leach harmful metals into your food, even when cooking acidic dishes like tamarind rasam or tomato chutney. This makes it a perfect choice for health-conscious cooks who don't want their cookware meddling with the nutritional integrity of their meals.

The enamel layer acts as a protective barrier, preventing iron from leaching into food—a common issue with uncoated cast iron. While a bit of extra iron might be beneficial for those with iron deficiencies, excessive intake can lead to health issues. With enamel-coated cast iron, you get the best of both worlds: the cooking benefits of cast iron without the risks.

High Heat? Bring It On!

Enamel-coated cast iron doesn't shy away from high heat, making it perfect for Indian cooking techniques like searing, frying, and tempering spices. Unlike non-stick pans, which break down at high temperatures, enamel-coated cast iron can handle the roaring flames of your tadka experiment without flinching. The enamel coating remains stable, ensuring no harmful substances are released into your food.

Imagine preparing a dish like palak paneer, where the paneer needs to be seared to golden perfection before being submerged in a creamy spinach gravy. A non-stick pan might fail you here, with its surface degrading under the high heat required for a good sear. Enamel-coated cast iron, on the other hand, gives you the perfect golden crust without compromising safety.

Built to Last (and Then Some)

If you've ever lamented the short lifespan of non-stick pans, enamel-coated cast iron will feel like a revelation. This cookware isn't just durable—it's practically indestructible. With proper care, it can last a lifetime (and often gets passed down through generations). Its resistance to wear and tear makes it a worthwhile investment, especially when compared to cheaper alternatives that need frequent replacement.

The initial cost might seem high, but think of it this way: how many scratched-up non-stick pans would you replace in the time it takes an enamel-coated cast iron pot to show its first signs of aging? Over its lifetime, this cookware pays for itself many times over, making it a cost-effective choice in the long run.

Easy to Clean, Easy to Love

While traditional cast iron requires regular seasoning to maintain its non-stick surface and prevent rust, enamel-coated cast iron is much more forgiving. The smooth enamel surface is easy to clean and doesn't require any special treatment—just wash it with warm water and mild soap, and you're good to go. Plus, it resists stains and doesn't absorb Flavors, making it ideal for the multi-cuisine enthusiast.

For instance, if you're switching from cooking a pungent fish curry to a mild vegetable pulao, you don't have to worry about lingering odours or Flavors. The enamel coating acts as a barrier, ensuring that each dish tastes exactly as it should.

Versatility Across the Board

One of the standout features of enamel-coated cast iron is its versatility. It transitions seamlessly from stovetop to oven, making it ideal for dishes that require a combination of cooking methods. Whether you're slow braising a lamb curry or baking a bhature dough, this cookware can handle it all.

Its aesthetic appeal is another bonus. Available in a variety of colours and finishes, enamel-coated cast iron looks as good on the dining table as it does on the stove. Hosting a dinner party? Serve your piping-hot biryani straight from the pot—it's functional and stylish.

The Perfect Partner for Indian Cuisine

Indian cooking often involves bold spices, tangy Flavors, and high heat, all of which demand resilient cookware. Enamel-coated cast iron checks every box, providing the durability, safety, and heat retention needed to handle complex recipes. Its non-reactive surface ensures that the vibrant Flavors of tamarind, chili, and turmeric remain untainted, preserving the authenticity of every dish.

Whether you're frying puris for a festive meal, simmering a slow-cooked stew for a family gathering, or preparing a quick stir-fry for weeknight dinner, enamel-coated cast iron proves itself time and again. It's the cookware equivalent of a multi-tasking genius—capable, reliable, and always ready for action.

Pure Titanium: The Lightweight Powerhouse

If there's one cookware material that sounds like it belongs in a sci-fi movie, it's titanium. But this isn't some futuristic gimmick—

it's a game-changing material for modern kitchens. Known for its strength, light weight, and non-reactivity, pure titanium cookware is a hero for those who value durability, versatility, and health in their cooking. While it may not have the nostalgic charm of cast iron or brass, its practical advantages are hard to ignore, especially in a fast-paced Indian kitchen.

Strength in Simplicity

Pure titanium is one of the strongest metals on Earth, yet it's surprisingly lightweight. This combination makes it ideal for cookware that needs to withstand high heat and regular use without being a pain to handle. Imagine tossing vegetables in a wok or lifting a kadhai full of biryani—titanium makes it all feel effortless.

Its toughness isn't just about resisting dents or scratches. Titanium is also non-reactive, which means it doesn't leach metals into your food, even when cooking acidic dishes like tomato-based curries or tamarind-heavy sambars. This sets it apart from stainless steel and aluminium, both of which can interact with ingredients and alter the taste—or worse, compromise your health.

The Health Halo

One of titanium's biggest selling points is its non-reactive nature. In an Indian kitchen, where tangy ingredients like lemons, tamarind, and tomatoes are staples, non-reactive cookware is essential. Unlike stainless steel, which can release nickel and chromium, or aluminium, which loves to bond with acids, titanium remains completely neutral. This means your imli chutney tastes just like it's supposed to—tangy and rich, with no metallic aftertaste.

For health-conscious cooks, titanium offers peace of mind. It's free from harmful chemicals like PTFE and PFAS (common in non-stick coatings), and it doesn't degrade over time, ensuring that your meals remain safe and uncontaminated.

High-Heat Hero

Titanium's heat tolerance is one of its standout features. It can handle the intense temperatures often required in Indian cooking without warping or releasing harmful substances. Whether you're frying puris, searing kebabs, or preparing a quick stir-fry, titanium cookware stays stable under pressure.

Picture this: you're frying bhaturas for a Sunday brunch. The oil needs to be at just the right temperature for the dough to puff up perfectly. With titanium cookware, you don't have to worry about uneven heating or overheating—its excellent thermal conductivity ensures consistent results every time.

Lightweight, Heavy on Performance

If you've ever struggled with lifting a cast iron pot full of hot curry, you'll appreciate titanium's feather-light feel. Despite its strength, titanium is incredibly light, making it easy to maneuver, even when you're juggling multiple dishes. It's particularly useful for stir-frying, where quick movements and high heat are key to getting the perfect texture and flavour.

This lightweight quality doesn't come at the expense of durability. Titanium is virtually indestructible, capable of withstanding daily use, high temperatures, and the occasional kitchen mishap without losing its shine—or its integrity. It's the cookware equivalent of a marathon runner: light on its feet but built to endure.

Easy Maintenance, No Fuss

Titanium cookware is a dream for those who dread cleaning up after a cooking session. Its smooth, non-porous surface makes it naturally non-stick, so food doesn't cling stubbornly to the pan. A quick rinse with warm water and mild soap is usually all it takes to clean up, even after frying or sautéing.

Unlike non-stick pans, which require delicate care and special utensils, titanium is tough enough to handle metal spatulas and whisks. You don't have to worry about scratching the surface or degrading its performance over time. It's cookware that works as hard as you do—without demanding constant upkeep.

Versatility That Matches Indian Cooking

Titanium's versatility makes it a valuable addition to any kitchen. It's equally adept at high-heat frying, gentle simmering, and everything in between. This makes it ideal for Indian cuisine, where a single meal might involve multiple cooking techniques.

For example, titanium excels at cooking acidic recipes like tomato-based curries or tamarind rasam, where other cookware might react or degrade. It's also perfect for quick, high-heat dishes like stir-fried vegetables, where speed and heat distribution are crucial. And if you're making something like kheer, where gentle, even heat is essential, titanium performs beautifully without scorching the milk.

An Investment Worth Making

Titanium cookware isn't the cheapest option on the market, but its durability and performance make it worth the investment. Unlike non-stick pans, which need to be replaced every few years, titanium cookware can last a lifetime. Its initial cost may be higher, but it pays for itself over time, both in longevity and in the health benefits of avoiding reactive metals or chemical coatings.

Think of it as a one-time investment in your kitchen's future. Instead of cycling through flimsy, disposable cookware, you get a reliable, long-lasting tool that enhances your cooking experience and protects your health.

The Perfect Partner for Everyday Cooking

Whether you're making a quick stir-fry, frying pakoras for a rainy day, or simmering a tangy tomato curry, titanium cookware is up to the task. Its combination of light weight, durability, and non-reactivity makes it a versatile choice for any home chef.

And let's not forget its aesthetic appeal. Titanium's sleek, modern look is a welcome addition to any kitchen, blending style with substance. It's cookware that doesn't just perform—it impresses.

Honourable Mentions: Alternatives to Consider

While enamel-coated cast iron and pure titanium are the undisputed heroes of the cookware world, a few other materials deserve a mention for their unique benefits. These options, though not without their quirks, can complement your kitchen arsenal and cater to specific cooking needs. Let's dive into these honourable mentions.

Glass Cookware: The Transparent Performer

Glass cookware is the unsung hero of the oven and microwave. Its non-reactive nature makes it perfect for dishes where purity of flavour is paramount, such as creamy baked pasta or delicate custards. Unlike metals, glass doesn't interact with acidic or alkaline foods, so your lemon soufflé stays zesty and untainted.

However, glass isn't without its challenges. It's fragile and prone to breaking if dropped or exposed to sudden temperature changes. The thought of a shattering glass dish mid-cooking is enough to give anyone pause. Additionally, glass doesn't handle high-heat stovetop cooking well, making it more of a specialist than an all-rounder.

Still, for baking, microwaving, or serving, glass cookware shines—both literally and figuratively.

Pre-Seasoned Cast Iron: The Traditional Powerhouse

For those who swear by the rich, earthy flavour of a perfectly seared steak or the crispy edges of a dosa, uncoated cast iron remains a kitchen classic. Its ability to retain heat is unparalleled, making it ideal for slow-cooking curries or frying crispy puris. Plus, as it ages, cast iron develops a natural non-stick surface through seasoning—a layer of polymerized fat that's both functional and nostalgic.

But uncoated cast iron isn't for everyone. It's heavy, requires regular maintenance to prevent rust, and can leach iron into food, which, while beneficial in small amounts, may not be ideal for everyone. Cooking acidic dishes like tomato-based curries can strip the seasoning and react with the iron, affecting both flavour and safety.

Despite these caveats, cast iron's robustness and heat retention make it a worthy addition to any kitchen—provided you're ready to commit to its care.

Ceramic Cookware: A Delicate Balance

While we've covered ceramic-coated cookware in-depth, pure ceramic cookware deserves a nod for its non-reactive properties and aesthetic appeal. Often handcrafted, ceramic pots and pans bring an artisanal touch to the kitchen, making them perfect for slow-cooked dishes like biryanis or stews.

The downside? They're delicate and prone to chipping. Ceramic isn't built for the high-heat drama of frying pakoras or making tadka, but for gentle, even cooking, it can hold its own. Just don't expect it to replace your heavy-duty pans.

The Price of Health: Why Quality Cookware is Worth the Investment

When it comes to cookware, the phrase "you get what you pay for" has never been truer. The allure of cheap, flashy non-stick pans or aluminium pots might tempt you, but over time, they reveal their flaws—wearing out, leaching harmful chemicals, and even ruining the flavour of your carefully prepared meals. On the other hand, investing in high-quality cookware like enamel-coated cast iron or pure titanium might feel like a stretch upfront, but it's a decision that pays dividends in health, convenience, and even financial savings. Let's delve into why premium cookware is a game-changer for your kitchen and life.

A Lifetime Companion, Not a Disposable Friend

The durability of premium cookware isn't just a selling point—it's a practical reality. Unlike non-stick pans that wear out within a couple of years, cookware made from materials like enamel-coated cast iron or pure titanium is built to last. These are the kinds of tools you can pass down to the next generation, not discard after a few scratch-filled months.

Imagine the savings: instead of replacing a subpar non-stick pan every two years, you invest once in a piece of cookware that accompanies you for decades. Yes, the upfront cost might feel hefty, but when spread across a lifetime, the price per use plummets. Think of it as the difference between fast fashion and timeless, tailored clothing.

Health is Wealth—And It's Priceless

Cheap cookware doesn't just take a toll on your wallet; it can also have a hidden cost on your health. Materials like Teflon-coated non-stick or aluminium may expose you to harmful chemicals, leaching metals, and even microplastics over time. These exposures add up, affecting your well-being in ways you may not immediately notice. Premium cookware, on the other hand, prioritizes safety.

- **Enamel-coated cast iron** doesn't leach chemicals or react with food, making it ideal for everything from acidic tomato curries to simmering dals.

- **Pure titanium**, lightweight and non-reactive, ensures that even high-heat stir-fries and tangy tamarind dishes remain pure and safe.

Switching to such materials isn't just about avoiding risks—it's about proactively choosing better health for yourself and your family. After all, what's the point of cooking nutritious food if the tools you're using compromise it?

Maintenance: So Easy, It's Almost Cheating

One of the biggest myths about premium cookware is that it's high maintenance. Sure, a traditional cast iron pan might need regular seasoning, but its enamel-coated cousin couldn't be simpler to care for. With just a soft sponge and mild soap, it's ready to go—no delicate handling or fussy care routines required.

Titanium cookware, too, is a dream to maintain. Its non-reactive surface resists stains and scratches, meaning you don't need to baby it. Forgot it on the stovetop for a few extra minutes? No problem— it can handle the heat without warping or degrading. And if you've ever spent 15 minutes scrubbing burnt bits off a low-quality pan, you'll appreciate how premium cookware saves you precious time and energy in the kitchen.

Flavors That Speak for Themselves

High-quality cookware doesn't just protect your health; it enhances the flavour of your food. The even heat distribution of enamel-coated cast iron allows spices to bloom and Flavors to meld beautifully, while titanium's rapid heating and non-reactivity ensure that delicate ingredients shine without interference. It's the kind of difference you notice in every bite—a richness and depth that's impossible to achieve with cheap, inconsistent cookware.

Even the simple act of making a tadka for dal transforms when your cookware works with you instead of against you. No uneven heating, no unwanted metallic tang—just pure, unadulterated flavour.

Long-Term Savings, Short-Term Joy

Yes, premium cookware comes with a higher price tag, but it's an investment that pays off in the long run. By avoiding frequent replacements and prioritizing health, you're saving money on both medical bills and constant cookware upgrades. Plus, many high-quality options come with lifetime warranties, giving you peace of mind that you'll never have to worry about replacements.

And the joy? There's something deeply satisfying about cooking with tools you trust—knowing that your cookware is designed to support your creativity, not sabotage it.

Matching the Right Cookware to Your Recipes

Every dish has its story, and every recipe deserves the right companion in the kitchen. The cookware you use isn't just a vessel; it's a partner in bringing out the Flavors, textures, and memories that make meals special. From slow-cooked dals to fiery stir-fries, choosing the right pan or pot ensures that every ingredient shines. Here's how to pair the cookware heroes we've uncovered with the recipes that define your cooking style.

Enamel-Coated Cast Iron: The Flavour Amplifier

For dishes that thrive on steady, even heat, enamel-coated cast iron is a champion. Its heat retention and non-reactive surface make it perfect for recipes that demand patience and depth of flavour.

- **Curries and Gravies:** Whether it's a rich butter chicken or a tangy tamarind fish curry, the even heat distribution ensures that every spice releases its full potential. The non-reactive enamel lining lets you simmer acidic ingredients like tomatoes and vinegar without worrying about leaching.

- **Slow-Cooked Stews:** A hearty mutton curry or vegetable stew benefits immensely from the steady warmth of cast iron. The thick walls allow Flavors to meld beautifully over low heat.

- **Dal Tadka:** The robust heat retention makes this the perfect vessel for tempering spices in hot oil and then pouring them over creamy lentils for that irresistible sizzle.

Pure Titanium: The Lightweight Powerhouse

When speed, high heat, and non-reactivity are the order of the day, titanium cookware steps in. Its quick heating and durability make it ideal for stir-fries and tangy recipes that might challenge other materials.

- **Stir-Fries and Sautés:** Whether tossing up a batch of chili paneer or a quick vegetable stir-fry, titanium heats up quickly and evenly, letting you lock in Flavors without delay.

- **Tomato-Based Dishes:** Think spicy rasam or a zingy tomato chutney. Titanium handles the acidity without breaking a sweat, ensuring a pure, clean taste.

- **High-Heat Frying:** For perfectly crispy pakoras or golden puris, titanium offers a safe, non-reactive surface that doesn't compromise on heat.

Stainless Steel (18/8 or 18/10): The Kitchen Workhorse

Stainless steel has its quirks, but when used for the right recipes, it's a reliable and durable ally. Its strength lies in high-heat and water-based cooking methods where metal reactivity isn't a concern.

- **Steaming and Boiling:** Whether you're steaming idlis, boiling pasta, or blanching vegetables, stainless steel pots excel at maintaining high temperatures without warping.

- **Soups and Broths:** From a simple tomato soup to a complex bone broth, stainless steel ensures that the ingredients cook evenly without altering the flavour.

- **Rice and Pulao:** Its non-reactive surface works well for preparing fluffy basmati rice or aromatic pulaos without any metallic aftertaste.

Glass Cookware: The Transparent Choice

Glass cookware may not be as versatile as the others, but for specific purposes, it's unmatched. Its non-reactive nature and ability to retain moisture make it a great choice for baking and microwaving.

- **Baking Delights:** Lasagnas, casseroles, and baked desserts like puddings and cakes turn out beautifully in glass. The even heat distribution ensures that every layer cooks to perfection.

- **Microwave Cooking:** For reheating or preparing quick dishes like a microwave dhokla, glass is a safe and practical option.

- **Storage and Presentation:** Glass doubles as a storage solution and serving dish, seamlessly transitioning from fridge to oven to table.

Honourable Mentions: When Specialty Matters

Some cookware pieces might not make the daily rotation but are invaluable for niche recipes.

- **Uncoated Cast Iron:** Ideal for searing meats, roasting vegetables, or making traditional dishes like appam or dosas. With proper seasoning, it becomes almost non-stick and adds a touch of iron to your meals.

- **Clay Pots:** For authentic, earthy Flavors, clay pots are unbeatable. Perfect for slow-cooking biryanis or making traditional dishes like khichdi.

- **Copper Cookware:** While its high reactivity makes it tricky, a lined copper vessel can be ideal for caramelizing sugar or preparing delicate sauces.

A Cookware Cheat Sheet for Everyday Use

Here's a quick guide to match your recipes with the perfect cookware:

Dish	Recommended Cookware	Why?
Curries and Gravies	Enamel-Coated Cast Iron	Even heat, non-reactive for acidic ingredients.
Stir-Fries and Sautés	Pure Titanium	Quick heating, durable, and handles high heat well.
Rice and Pulao	Stainless Steel (18/8 or 18/10)	Non-reactive, evenly cooks grains.
Soups and Broths	Stainless Steel (18/10)	Ideal for water-based recipes, no metal leaching.
Fried Foods (Pakoras)	Pure Titanium	Handles high heat and prevents oil sticking.
Lasagnas and Casseroles	Glass Cookware	Moisture retention and even baking.
Appam/Dosas	Uncoated Cast Iron	Natural non-stick surface with proper seasoning.

By understanding how cookware interacts with ingredients and cooking methods, you not only elevate your dishes but also maximize the lifespan and safety of your kitchen tools. It's not about filling your shelves with every material—it's about choosing the right tools for the meals that matter most to you.

Chapter 3

The Oil Slick – Choosing Fats That Won't Let You Down

The Oil Aisle Drama – What Are We Even Buying?

The Marketing Circus

Wandering into the cooking oil aisle should be a straightforward task, but it often feels like stepping into a marketing circus. Each bottle competes for your attention with flashy claims and buzzwords, leaving you wondering whether you're buying oil or auditioning it for a leading role in a health documentary. "Heart-healthy," "cold-pressed," "light," "cholesterol-free"—it's a vocabulary explosion that does little to clarify and everything to confuse. And let's not forget the bottles that promise a near-spiritual experience: golden labels with words like "virgin" and "pure" glowing like a halo. At this point, you half-expect an oil to cure all diseases and babysit your kids.

Take the "cholesterol-free" label, for instance. Here's a fact nobody tells you: all plant-based oils are naturally cholesterol-free. So why the big announcement on every bottle? It's like labelling water "wet"—true but entirely unnecessary. Then there's "light," a word that seems to promise fewer calories or at least some magical slimming effect on your cooking. Spoiler alert: it's neither. "Light" simply means it's low on flavour, which, depending on your dish, might be a complete disaster. Imagine frying samosas and ending up with food that tastes like sadness dipped in air.

And then comes "cold-pressed," the crown jewel of modern health marketing. It conjures up idyllic visions of fresh seeds delicately squeezed at a serene Himalayan monastery. In reality, it just means the oil wasn't exposed to heat during extraction. Sure, that retains some nutrients, but does it justify a price tag that feels like a personal insult? Probably not. Yet, the combination of "cold" and "pressed" somehow makes us reach for it, convinced we're making the noblest choice.

Oil companies know exactly what they're doing. They prey on three types of guilt we all have: health guilt, wallet guilt, and FOMO guilt. The first tells you to fry less because, let's face it, you'll eat more. The second makes you hesitate at the fancy oils, wondering why mustard oil costs pennies compared to that sleek avocado oil. And the third whispers, "Don't you want the oil everyone's raving about?" The result? An overthinking spiral that ends with you grabbing the bottle that looks the least terrifying.

I remember standing in an aisle once, gripping two bottles of olive oil. One was "extra-virgin," and the other claimed to be "extra-light." I stared at them, trying to decipher their hidden meaning. Was one healthier? Tastier? Was I about to shame myself for years with the wrong choice? Eventually, I Googled it right there in the aisle. Turns out, "extra-virgin" means the oil's pure and unprocessed, while "extra-light" is just stripped of flavour and colour. In other words, the olive oil equivalent of wearing beige. I left with both bottles and a newfound understanding of how oils can gaslight you into thinking you're the problem.

And then there's the myth of "heart-healthy" oils. This label is everywhere, promising you a long life and a cholesterol level your doctor will applaud. Here's the catch: many oils labelled "heart-healthy" are rich in omega-3s, which is great. But to actually benefit, you'd need to consume absurd amounts, basically drinking oil like its water. What they don't tell you is that heavily refined oils, even those labelled healthy, are often stripped of most nutrients during processing. What you're left with is a nutrient-deprived fat delivery system—perfect for frying but hardly the elixir of health the label implies.

The truth is that oil marketing thrives on confusion. They throw jargon at you, hoping you'll surrender and buy what seems the least offensive. But the key to choosing the right oil isn't in the marketing—it's in understanding how you'll use it. Is it for frying? Go for something stable at high heat. For drizzling? Pick an unrefined one with flavour. Everything else, from "cholesterol-free" to "light," is just noise designed to make you doubt yourself.

The Science of Fats: What's the Big Fat Deal?

Fats. The very word triggers mixed emotions—joy when it's on a buttery paratha, guilt when it's part of a samosa binge, and confusion when you're staring at a shelf lined with "low-fat," "omega-rich," and "cold-pressed" oils. But here's the thing: fats aren't just blobs on your food pyramid—they're crucial, sneaky players in your diet, impacting everything from your energy levels to your heart health.

Let's start with the essentials. You've got good fats—monounsaturated and polyunsaturated ones. These are like the friends who not only show up on time but bring snacks to share. Found in olive oil, nuts, seeds, and fatty fish, they're famous for lowering bad cholesterol, fighting inflammation, and keeping your heart happy. Then, lurking in the dark corner of your plate, are bad fats—the trans fats. These impostors are found in margarine, packaged snacks, and deep-fried regrets. They sneakily boost your bad cholesterol (LDL), tank the good cholesterol (HDL), and cause inflammation, leaving your arteries to deal with the aftermath.

And in the middle of this spectrum are the much-maligned saturated fats. For years, they've been typecast as villains, clogging arteries and ruining hearts. But new science suggests a more nuanced view. Turns out, not all saturated fats are equal. Ghee and coconut oil, for instance, have shorter fatty acid chains, making them easier to digest and even helpful for quick energy bursts. Saturated fats aren't saints, but in moderation, they're not the dietary devils they were once made out to be.

Now, about those omega fats. If you've heard terms like omega-3 and omega-6 tossed around like they're some exclusive club, here's the lowdown. Omega-3s, found in fish, flaxseeds, and walnuts, are the anti-inflammatory warriors we all need. They protect the heart, keep joints happy, and boost brainpower. Omega-6s, found in vegetable oils like sunflower and soybean, are also essential, but too much of them can wreak havoc. Picture omega-3 and omega-6 as siblings—things are great when they're balanced, but too much omega-6 can turn a healthy family meal into a never-ending sibling rivalry, fuelling inflammation and chronic diseases.

And let's not forget about the drama of smoke points. Every fat has a limit, a temperature at which it starts to smoke, degrade, and become downright toxic. Extra-virgin olive oil, beloved in the Mediterranean, has a low smoke point, making it a terrible choice for Indian tadkas. Ghee, on the other hand, thrives in high-heat situations, as does mustard oil—just make sure you heat it properly to temper its pungency before adding other ingredients. Oils that break down under heat not only lose flavour but also invite harmful free radicals to your plate.

It doesn't help that the marketing world is out to confuse us. Terms like "light oil," "low-fat," and "cholesterol-free" are plastered on bottles like badges of honour. Fun fact: all plant-based oils are naturally cholesterol-free because only animal products contain cholesterol. Meanwhile, "light" oil isn't a calorie-reduced miracle—

it's just been stripped of its flavour and nutrients through processing. And while we're on buzzwords, "heart-healthy" doesn't always mean what you think. Some oils are marketed as heart-friendly despite being high in omega-6 or refined beyond recognition.

To add to the chaos, fats also play tricks on our taste buds and brains. They're why sautéed onions smell irresistible, why curries feel indulgent, and why crispy pakoras are worth the calories. Our bodies are hardwired to crave fats because they signal energy and satiety. But there's a fine line between enjoying a buttery naan and turning every meal into a grease-fest. It's a delicate dance, one that requires a little restraint and a lot of awareness.

The solution? Think of fats as a buffet. Rotate your options—ghee for frying, olive oil for drizzling, coconut oil for sautéing—and reap the benefits of variety. Each fat brings its own nutrients and flavour profile, so mixing things up keeps your meals both interesting and balanced. Over-relying on one oil, no matter how healthy it seems, can tip the scales in the wrong direction. Think of it as spreading out the workload among friends: no one oil needs to bear the entire weight of your culinary ambitions.

And portion control? Crucial. A tablespoon here and a dollop there can add up faster than you realize. Fats are calorie-dense, and while they make food taste divine, moderation ensures they don't overshadow the dish—or your health. Let fats play their part as the supporting cast, enhancing the Flavors without stealing the spotlight.

Without fuss or guilt, fats deserve a place on your plate and in your cooking routine. After all, they're the reason food transforms from a chore to a pleasure. Whether it's the richness of ghee on a dal, the crispiness of mustard oil in pakoras, or the subtle warmth of coconut oil in a curry, fats are the silent artists behind every delicious bite. And with a little knowledge, you can use them to create magic in the kitchen, one glorious spoonful at a time.

Refined Oils: A Factory, Not a Farm

If oils could talk, refined ones would probably have a dark, twisted memoir to share. Picture this: a sunflower seed starts its life basking in golden fields, full of potential to nourish and flavour our food. But before it can fulfil its wholesome destiny, it's tossed into the mechanical equivalent of a dystopian factory. What emerges isn't the vibrant essence of the seed but a pale, overly polished, shadow of its former self. Welcome to the world of refined oils—a place where nutritional dreams go to die and marketing spin flourishes.

The refining process is a masterclass in stripping oils of everything natural and adding a few surprises you never asked for. First, raw materials like soybeans, sunflower seeds, or corn kernels are squeezed, but mechanical pressing alone doesn't get enough oil. So, out comes the chemical cavalry, with solvents like hexane that suck every last drop. If you're imagining gentle farmhands and artisanal techniques, erase that mental image. This process is industrial to the core.

The oil is now a cloudy, smelly, slightly grotesque liquid that no consumer in their right mind would buy. So, the refining process begins. High heat is applied to bleach out the colour, neutralize the odour, and make the oil "shelf stable." It's deodorized to remove any trace of its original ingredients, leaving you with an ultra-neutral oil that could pass for a culinary ghost. If you've ever wondered why refined oils taste like nothing, it's because everything—even their soul—has been boiled, bleached, and blasted away.

By the time the refining process is complete, what's left is a product that looks clean but is essentially empty. Antioxidants, vitamins, and phytonutrients—those tiny warriors that help fight free radicals in your body—are among the casualties. What's gained? A product with a long shelf life and no discernible character. Think of it as the oil version of a plastic apple—immortal but utterly pointless for nourishment.

The true villains of refined oils lie in what's added during this process or formed as byproducts. Some refined oils may contain residual traces of the chemical solvents used during extraction, like hexane. While industry experts argue that these traces are negligible, the idea of consuming even a whisper of industrial solvent isn't exactly comforting. Then there are trans fats. These nasties can form during the high-heat deodorization process, especially if the oil isn't carefully managed. Trans fats are the uninvited guests at your table, bringing with them inflammation, heart disease, and a VIP pass to your arteries.

Refined oils are also notorious for their high omega-6 content, and while omega-6 fatty acids aren't inherently evil, balance is everything. Modern diets, especially in countries like India, are already drowning in omega-6 from refined oils, processed foods, and snacks. An excess of these fats relative to omega-3s tilts the balance toward inflammation, increasing risks for heart disease, diabetes, and even mental health issues. It's like inviting too many rowdy guests to a party—they dominate the conversation and make everything worse.

The irony is that refined oils are marketed as "light" and "healthy," thanks to their neutral flavour and cholesterol-free nature. Never mind that plants don't have cholesterol in the first place—slapping a "cholesterol-free" label on a bottle of sunflower oil is about as meaningful as advertising "oxygen-free" concrete. It's a distraction from the real issues, like the oil's lack of nutrition or the free radicals it may carry from being overheated.

Refined oils often play the role of "filler oils" in blended products. Ever noticed that bottle claiming to be "pure" or "natural" but with a suspiciously low price? Check the fine print—it's likely a mix of refined oils diluted with something cheaper. These blends are perfectly legal, but they turn your cooking oil into a Frankenstein mix of unclear origins. If your oil bottle reads more like a chemistry textbook than a food label, it's time to rethink your purchase.

And yet, refined oils persist in nearly every kitchen. Why? They're cheap, stable, and can withstand high-heat cooking. Their neutral taste means they don't interfere with the Flavors of your dish—perfect if you're frying fish one day and making jalebis the next. But convenience has its costs, and in this case, it's your health.

The good news is that you don't have to banish refined oils entirely, but moderation is key. If deep-frying is a once-a-month indulgence, using a refined oil with a high smoke point, like rice bran or sunflower oil, won't do irreparable damage. The issue arises when these oils dominate your cooking routine, sneaking into every sabzi, curry, and paratha you make. That's when the long-term effects—nutritional deficiencies, inflammation, and the cumulative burden of free radicals—start to show.

For those committed to moving beyond refined oils, cold-pressed alternatives offer a lifeline. Cold-pressed oils retain their natural antioxidants, Flavors, and colours because they're extracted using mechanical methods at lower temperatures. They're less processed, less likely to contain chemical residues, and far more flavourful. However, they come with limitations: a shorter shelf life, lower smoke points, and a price tag that can make you wince. But think of it as an investment in your health and your food's flavour. After all, isn't it better to use a tablespoon of flavourful oil that elevates your dish than drown it in a bland, over-processed counterpart?

The takeaway here isn't to vilify refined oils entirely. For all their sins, they're undeniably versatile, especially for high-heat applications where other oils might falter. The goal is to strike a balance—use them sparingly, avoid reusing fried oil, and pair them with nutrient-rich ingredients to mitigate their deficiencies. Better yet, diversify your oil stash: let cold-pressed oils, ghee, and mustard oil have a say in your kitchen too.

Cold-Pressed Comeback

Cold-pressed oils have strutted back into the limelight like a retro trend that somehow manages to feel fresh again. Imagine your grandparents looking smug as they watch these artisanal oils fly off the shelves—because, let's be honest, they've been swearing by this stuff for decades. Long before Instagram food bloggers touted the benefits of "virgin coconut oil" or "organic mustard oil," cold-pressed oils were a staple in every desi kitchen. And now, with health-conscious eaters everywhere rejecting the chemical-laden chaos of refined oils, these nutrient-packed gems are enjoying their much-deserved renaissance.

The charm of cold-pressed oils lies in their simplicity. No high-heat extraction. No industrial chemicals. No solvents with names so long they sound like a pharmaceutical prescription. The process is exactly what it says on the tin: oil extracted by pressing seeds or nuts at low temperatures. It's straightforward, preserving the natural Flavors, nutrients, and colours that make these oils stand out from their refined cousins.

Take coconut oil, for instance. The cold-pressed version retains a rich, nutty aroma and a snow-white hue that practically screams "purity." Ghee, when made using traditional methods, captures the buttery essence and golden sheen that elevate a dish from tasty to heavenly. Even mustard oil—peppery, intense, and unapologetically bold—feels alive in its cold-pressed form, packing a punch that refined versions dilute to bland mediocrity.

But cold-pressed oils aren't just about taste; they're nutrient powerhouses. Unlike refined oils, which lose their antioxidants, vitamins, and fatty acids during processing, cold-pressed oils come brimming with all the good stuff. These oils are high in polyphenols—antioxidants that help fight inflammation and oxidative stress—and retain essential fatty acids that your body loves. Plus, their natural extraction process ensures they don't harbour the chemical residues or free radicals often found in refined oils.

Of course, no food fad escapes its limitations, and cold-pressed oils are no exception. For starters, they have a lower smoke point than refined oils, meaning they can't handle the screaming-hot temperatures of deep-frying. Forget about dunking your samosas into a pan of cold-pressed olive oil—it'll smoke up your kitchen faster than a failed tadka attempt. These oils are best suited for medium-heat cooking or, better yet, as finishing oils that drizzle over salads, soups, or grilled vegetables.

Then there's the cost. Cold-pressed oils can be pricey, and if you're not careful, you might find yourself hesitating to pour more than a teaspoon. It's a far cry from the carefree glugs of refined oil we're used to, but think of it as a luxury investment—like a bottle of fine wine, except it doesn't give you a headache the next day. The richness and depth these oils bring to your dishes make the splurge worthwhile.

But here's the real reason cold-pressed oils are back in the game: people are craving authenticity. In a world where processed, mass-produced foods dominate, these oils offer a connection to simpler, more honest cooking. They remind us that food isn't just fuel— it's an experience, steeped in culture, flavour, and care. The act of cooking with a fragrant, golden stream of cold-pressed sesame oil feels special, as if you're paying homage to generations of home cooks who knew the value of quality ingredients.

What's more, cold-pressed oils are making their way into modern kitchens without losing their traditional roots. Take South Indian households, where cold-pressed coconut oil has long been a go-to for tempering spices in sambar or adding richness to a stew. Or Bengali kitchens, where mustard oil lends its fiery personality to fish curries and pickles. These oils don't just cook food; they tell stories of regions, rituals, and recipes passed down through time.

So, when should you use cold-pressed oils? The answer lies in balance and intention. Use them where their distinct Flavors can shine. Drizzle cold-pressed sesame oil over your noodles for an earthy finish. Add a spoonful of cold-pressed coconut oil to your curries for that tropical kick. Let cold-pressed mustard oil take centre stage in a mustard fish curry, where its boldness is part of the charm.

But don't waste these oils where they don't belong. High-heat frying is their nemesis. Not only will the heat obliterate their delicate Flavors, but it can also degrade the beneficial compounds you paid a premium for. If your recipe calls for frying, stick to refined oils or ghee and save your cold-pressed treasures for lighter cooking or finishing touches.

Another pro tip: store cold-pressed oils properly. Their natural extraction process makes them more vulnerable to spoilage, so keep them in cool, dark places and seal them tightly. Avoid the heartbreak of rancid oil—it's like discovering your favourite outfit shrunk in the wash. Trust us, a little care goes a long way.

Cold-pressed oils are a reminder that not all progress means betterment. Sometimes, the old ways—the slow, deliberate, handcrafted methods—are worth revisiting. They offer a chance to savour food as it was meant to be, unadulterated and alive with flavour. So, the next time you see a bottle of cold-pressed mustard oil or coconut oil sitting on the shelf, don't just glance at the price tag and walk away. Think of the stories, the care, and the craftsmanship that went into making it. Then, bring it home and let it remind you why good food starts with good ingredients

Indian Oils – Tradition or Trend?

Ghee: The Golden Villain-Turned-Hero

Ghee, once considered the culinary equivalent of a guilty pleasure, has somehow staged the most dramatic comeback since bell-bottom jeans. For decades, it bore the brunt of every cholesterol-lowering campaign, cast aside in favour of lighter, "modern" alternatives. But as the science of nutrition catches up with our ancestors' wisdom, ghee has gone from dietary villain to golden hero. Ayurveda always knew it, your dadi (grandmother) always insisted on it, and now, even nutritionists are admitting it: ghee is liquid gold—both in colour and in benefits.

Let's start with the basics. Ghee is clarified butter, which means its butter stripped of its water content and milk solids. What's left is pure fat with a nutty aroma and a rich, almost caramel-like taste that makes everything it touches a little more indulgent. Whether it's dolloped onto a bowl of steaming dal or melted into a paratha fresh off the tawa, ghee transforms simple ingredients into memorable meals.

But it's not just flavour that makes ghee stand out. Nutritionally, it's a powerhouse. Rich in fat-soluble vitamins like A, D, E, and K, ghee helps your body absorb essential nutrients. It's also packed with butyric acid, a short-chain fatty acid that supports gut health and reduces inflammation. The best part? Ghee has a high smoke point—around 250°C—which makes it perfect for Indian cooking techniques like frying, roasting, and tempering spices. Unlike other oils that break down and release harmful compounds at high heat, ghee remains stable, letting you crank up the flame without a second thought.

Of course, ghee isn't just about nutrition. In Indian culture, it's practically sacred. From being used in religious rituals to starring in festive feasts, ghee is more than just an ingredient—it's a symbol of prosperity and love. When dadi insists on adding an extra spoonful to your plate, it's not just for taste; it's her way of saying, "I care."

But let's address the elephant in the room: fat. For years, ghee was demonized for being high in saturated fat, with every health magazine warning us to steer clear. It didn't matter that generations before us thrived on ghee-laden diets. But science has flipped the narrative. Research now shows that moderate consumption of ghee, especially in the context of a balanced diet, poses no significant threat to heart health. In fact, the short-chain fatty acids in ghee are easier to digest than long-chain ones found in many other fats, making it a healthier choice than we were led to believe.

So how should you use ghee in your kitchen? The answer is: everywhere, but wisely. Its high smoke point makes it ideal for frying and tempering spices, adding depth to everything from dal tadka to biryanis. Use it to roast vegetables for a caramelized finish or spread it on hot rotis for a taste of nostalgia. A small spoonful can even elevate desserts like halwa, lending them a richness that's hard to replicate.

That said, ghee is a concentrated fat, so portion control is key. A dollop is delightful, but overindulgence can quickly tip the scales—literally. Think of ghee as a flavour enhancer rather than a cooking base. A teaspoon here, a tablespoon there, and suddenly, your dish has gone from good to "pass the recipe, please!"

There's also the question of quality. Not all ghee is created equal. The best ghee comes from grass-fed cows and is prepared using traditional methods, where the milk is cultured into curd, churned into butter, and then clarified. This process not only enhances the flavour but also retains more nutrients. So, while you might find jars of "pure ghee" at every grocery store, take a closer look at the label. Better yet, try making it at home—it's simpler than you think and infinitely more satisfying.

In a world obsessed with trendy superfoods, ghee is proof that sometimes, the real heroes are the ones we've known all along. It's not just a cooking fat; it's a piece of our culinary identity, a link to our roots, and a testament to the wisdom of traditional Indian kitchens. So, the next time someone asks if you'd like a little extra ghee, say yes. Not just because it's delicious, but because it's a reminder that good food—and good health—often starts with the simplest of ingredients.

Mustard Oil: Bold, Beautiful, and Misunderstood

There's no mistaking mustard oil when it walks into the room—or the kitchen. With its deep golden hue and sharp, peppery aroma, it's the oil equivalent of a fiery protagonist: unmissable, unapologetic, and unforgettable. For generations, mustard oil has been a staple in Indian households, especially in Bengal, Punjab, and Rajasthan, where its pungency is celebrated rather than muted. Yet, in the modern kitchen, it's often overlooked—sometimes even shunned—thanks to a combination of misinformation and changing culinary trends.

First, let's get one thing straight: mustard oil is not for the faint of heart. It's an oil that announces itself, with a bite that can make bland ingredients sing. Fry your pakoras in it, and they'll come out with a depth of flavour that regular vegetable oils simply can't achieve. Use it in pickles, and you'll see why it's the backbone of every tangy, spicy achar you've ever loved. From sautéing mustard greens to finishing off fish curries, mustard oil doesn't just enhance dishes—it defines them.

But why does this bold oil come with such a mixed reputation? A large part of the confusion stems from its erucic acid content, which has sparked debates about its safety for human consumption. Back in the day, studies suggested that erucic acid might pose risks to heart health, particularly when consumed in large quantities. These findings led some countries to restrict its use as an edible oil, branding mustard oil as "for external use only." The irony? Millions of Indians continued cooking with it, living long, flavourful lives in the process.

Modern research has nuanced the story. While excessive consumption of erucic acid might be harmful, the moderate amounts typically used in Indian diets pose little to no risk for healthy individuals. Moreover, mustard oil boasts an impressive nutrient profile: it's rich in monounsaturated and polyunsaturated fats, particularly omega-3 and omega-6 fatty acids, which are known to support heart health, reduce inflammation, and improve brain function. Add its natural antibacterial and antifungal properties, and you've got an oil that's as functional as it is flavourful.

Beyond health, mustard oil's cultural significance can't be ignored. In many Indian households, it's more than just an ingredient—it's a tradition. A wedding without mustard oil in the rituals? Unthinkable. A grandmother's kitchen without its signature scent? Unimaginable. In Bengali cuisine, mustard oil is almost sacred, lending its robust character to classics like shorshe ilish (hilsa fish in mustard sauce) and alu posto (potatoes in poppy seed paste). It's a reminder of roots, of family meals, and of a time when cooking wasn't just about sustenance but about storytelling.

Using mustard oil, however, comes with its own set of rules. The most important one? Always heat it first. Mustard oil has a raw, biting taste when uncooked, which can overpower a dish. Heating it to its smoking point not only tempers this intensity but also enhances its flavour. Once it's hot and aromatic, you can use it for frying, tempering, or even as a finishing oil to drizzle over cooked vegetables.

So where does mustard, oil shine the brightest? Pretty much anywhere high heat and bold Flavors are called for. Frying fish? Mustard oil gives it a crisp, golden crust that pairs beautifully with its peppery undertone. Making pickles? Its natural preservative properties keep them fresh and flavourful for months. Stir-frying vegetables or meats? Mustard oil adds a complexity that elevates even the simplest of stir-fries. It's versatile enough for everything from deep-frying pakoras to lightly sautéing greens, yet distinctive enough to stand out in every dish it touches.

But mustard oil isn't just for cooking. Its versatility extends to wellness rituals, skincare, and even hair care. Got a cough or cold? A mustard oil massage, warmed with a hint of garlic or ajwain (carom seeds), is a time-honoured remedy. Dry scalp or brittle hair? Mustard oil works wonders as a natural conditioner, leaving hair soft, shiny, and nourished. It's this multi-purpose magic that has kept mustard oil relevant across generations, even as other oils have come and gone.

Of course, like all good things, moderation is key. Mustard oil is potent—both in flavour and in its nutrient density. A little goes a long way, so it's best used as part of a balanced rotation with other cooking fats. Whether it's paired with the nutty richness of ghee or the creamy smoothness of coconut oil, mustard oil brings a counterpoint that keeps meals interesting and flavourful.

For those still hesitant to embrace mustard oil, consider this: every culture has its bold, defining Flavors. The French have their butter. The Italians have their olive oil. Indians? We have mustard oil—unapologetically bold, uniquely ours, and capable of turning any dish into a masterpiece. It's not just an oil; it's a celebration of flavour, tradition, and the unapologetic joy of cooking.

So, heat that kadhai, pour in the mustard oil, and let it smoke. What follows isn't just cooking—it's a legacy in motion. A legacy that's bold, beautiful, and, once you get to know it, utterly indispensable.

Coconut Oil: From Frying to Hair Care

Coconut oil is the overachiever of oils, seamlessly straddling the worlds of cooking, skincare, and even social media trends. South Indians have known its magic for centuries, but the rest of the world? They're only just catching up, slathering it on toast, swirling it in coffee, and dubbing it the ultimate superfood. And why not? Coconut oil brings an intoxicating aroma, unmatched versatility, and a health profile that puts most other oils to shame.

In a South Indian kitchen, coconut oil isn't just an ingredient; it's the soul of the cuisine. The aroma of sizzling curry leaves in hot coconut oil is a sensory experience that no pre-packaged spice mix can replicate. Whether it's a rich avial, a fiery Chettinad curry, or the simplest Kerala-style fish fry, coconut oil doesn't just blend in— it dominates, unapologetically tying the dish to its tropical roots. That's the thing about coconut oil: it's as much about identity as it is about flavour.

But what makes this oil such a darling in the culinary world? For one, its stability. Coconut oil is packed with saturated fats, which makes it one of the most stable oils for cooking. It has a smoke point of about 177°C, meaning it holds its structure well at medium to high heat. This makes it perfect for sautéing spices, tempering dals, and frying vadas without the risk of harmful compounds forming. And let's talk about deep-frying—coconut oil's ability to crisp up snacks while infusing them with its subtle nuttiness is practically unmatched.

Of course, the term "saturated fat" has been the oil's Achilles' heel, giving it a bad rap during the low-fat craze of the 90s and early 2000s. Back then, every health guru worth their oat bran would have you believe coconut oil was a one-way ticket to clogged arteries. But modern research has been kinder. Turns out, not all saturated fats are created equal. The medium-chain triglycerides (MCTs) in coconut oil are metabolized differently from the long-chain fatty acids in animal fats. These MCTs are easily digested, quickly converted into energy, and less likely to be stored as body fat.

Coconut oil is also rich in lauric acid, a fatty acid with antibacterial, antiviral, and antifungal properties. This makes it a superstar not just for your gut but also for your skin and hair. Yes, your mom was right all along—coconut oil as a pre-wash hair treatment genuinely works. And that's not all. Got dry skin? Coconut oil. Chapped lips? Coconut oil. A dosa pan that's a bit too sticky? You guessed it—coconut oil.

But it's not all roses—or coconuts. While its tropical aroma is beloved in South Indian cooking, it doesn't always play nice with every cuisine. Try tossing pasta in coconut oil, and it'll taste like your Italian nonna accidentally vacationed in Goa. For Indian dishes outside the coastal belt, the flavour of coconut oil can be overpowering. Imagine using it in a Punjabi makhani gravy; the clash of creamy tomato and coconut can be, well, distracting.

That's why coconut oil works best in dishes where its personality can shine. Coconut curries, seafood stews, and fried snacks are where it truly thrives. It's also a natural partner for tempering—those mustard seeds, curry leaves, and dried chilies simply love dancing in its heat. And for baking? Swap butter for coconut oil in cookies or cakes for a hint of tropical flair.

But not all coconut oils are created equal. If you're buying the refined stuff, you're missing out on its real magic. Refined coconut oil is bleached, deodorized, and stripped of its signature aroma. It's the introverted cousin to extra-virgin coconut oil, which retains all its natural goodness and that beautiful, nutty scent. Extra-virgin coconut oil is cold pressed from fresh coconuts, preserving its nutrients and flavour. It's pricier, sure, but for most dishes, it's worth the splurge.

That said, coconut oil has its limits. Its medium smoke point makes it unsuitable for extremely high heat cooking like deep-frying samosas or making a tadka for robust dals. For these, ghee or mustard oil are better choices. Coconut oil also tends to solidify in cooler climates, which is a feature, not a bug—it's just nature's way of telling you it's the real deal. A quick warm-up in the microwave or on the stove, and you're good to go.

For the health-conscious crowd, coconut oil has become something of a wellness mascot. It's slathered on everything from gluten-free pancakes to paleo granola bars, hailed as a metabolism booster and energy source. While these claims are grounded in the unique benefits of MCTs, it's important to remember that coconut oil is still a fat, packing nine calories per gram. Moderation is key, whether you're frying fish or blending it into your bulletproof coffee.

In Indian households, coconut oil's appeal goes beyond its culinary uses. It's a pantry workhorse that moonlights as a beauty product, a home remedy, and even a polish for wooden utensils. Its versatility makes it indispensable, whether you're moisturizing your elbows or greasing a stubborn idli mold. It's no wonder that for many, the scent of coconut oil isn't just comforting—it's nostalgic, evoking memories of home-cooked meals and childhood hair massages.

Ultimately, coconut oil is more than just a cooking medium; it's a lifestyle. It reminds us of the wisdom of our ancestors, who understood the value of natural, multi-functional ingredients long before the world caught on. So, the next time you open a jar of coconut oil, take a moment to appreciate its journey—from the palm-lined shores of Kerala to your frying pan. Whether you're tempering a sambar or taming a bad hair day, coconut oil is proof that sometimes, the simplest ingredients are the most extraordinary.

Fancy Foreigners in the Kitchen

Olive Oil: The Diva

Olive oil is like the celebrity chef of cooking fats—always in the spotlight, endlessly praised, and carrying an aura of Mediterranean sophistication. Every bottle of extra-virgin olive oil on the shelf seems to whisper promises of health, longevity, and the ability to pull off a Greek salad with style. But for all its glamour, olive oil can be a bit of a diva, especially when you try to make it do something it wasn't designed for—like frying pakoras or tempering spices.

The journey of olive oil from groves to grocery shelves is a tale of meticulous care. The best extra-virgin olive oils are cold-pressed, meaning they're extracted without heat or chemicals, preserving their flavour and nutrients. The result? A rich, fruity, peppery liquid gold that chefs and foodies rave about. But for the average Indian kitchen, where frying and high-heat cooking reign supreme, olive oil can feel like a guest who refuses to adapt to local customs.

Here's the thing about olive oil: it's not just one oil. It's a family, with members ranging from extra-virgin to refined to pomace. Extra-virgin olive oil is the star—the purest, least processed, and most flavourful. It's perfect for salads, drizzling on hummus, or even dipping bread. Virgin olive oil is a slightly less exclusive sibling, great for low-heat cooking. Refined olive oil, which has been processed to neutralize its flavour and increase its smoke point, is more practical for cooking. And then there's pomace olive oil, made from the leftover pulp after pressing. It's cheap, functional, and about as glamorous as a leftover chapati.

The health benefits of olive oil are legendary, and they're not just marketing fluff. Packed with monounsaturated fats and antioxidants, extra-virgin olive oil has been shown to support heart health, reduce inflammation, and even improve brain function. The Mediterranean diet, which treats olive oil like a culinary cornerstone, is often cited as one of the healthiest eating patterns in the world. But here's where it gets tricky: while olive oil shines in salads and sautés, it doesn't perform as well in an Indian kitchen where smoke points matter.

The smoke point of extra-virgin olive oil is around 160°C, which is low compared to other cooking fats. This means it starts breaking down at a relatively low temperature, releasing free radicals and losing its nutritional benefits. Try frying puris or making a tadka with extra-virgin olive oil, and you'll end up with a kitchen full of smoke and a dish that tastes faintly of burnt grass. For high-heat cooking, refined olive oil is a better choice, but even then, it lacks the robustness of ghee or mustard oil.

Flavour is another reason olive oil doesn't always fit into Indian cooking. Its fruity, slightly bitter notes can clash with the earthy, spicy Flavors of traditional Indian dishes. Imagine pouring extra-virgin olive oil over a plate of rajma chawal. It's a culinary culture shock no one asked for. Olive oil works best when it's allowed to be itself, enhancing Mediterranean dishes, light stir-fries, or even pasta sauces. In these settings, its flavour feels like a natural extension of the ingredients.

But let's give olive oil credit where it's due. Its versatility in global cuisine is unmatched. A drizzle of good-quality extra-virgin olive oil can elevate roasted vegetables, transform a simple piece of bread, or add richness to soups and stews. It's a natural partner for herbs, cheese, and tomatoes, making it indispensable in Western-style cooking. And when it comes to salad dressings, olive oil is the undisputed champion, blending effortlessly with vinegar, lemon juice, or mustard to create magic.

For those trying to incorporate olive oil into their Indian kitchen, the key is moderation and purpose. Use extra-virgin olive oil as a finishing touch for warm naan or drizzle it over roasted eggplant. Opt for refined olive oil when cooking at medium heat, like sautéing veggies or making a light curry. And don't even think about deep-frying samosas in it—olive oil wasn't built for that kind of abuse.

Of course, no discussion of olive oil is complete without addressing its price tag. A bottle of high-quality extra-virgin olive oil can cost as much as a small grocery haul. And while it's worth it for its flavour and health benefits, it's not exactly economical for households that cook multiple meals a day. For most Indian kitchens, olive oil is more of a specialty ingredient than an everyday staple.

Still, olive oil's popularity in India is growing, driven by health-conscious consumers and the increasing influence of Western cuisine. Many households now keep a bottle of olive oil on hand for specific uses, like making pasta or dressing salads. And while it may never replace ghee or mustard oil as a kitchen essential, it's carving out its own niche as a symbol of modern, global cooking.

Ultimately, olive oil is like a pair of designer shoes—impressive, luxurious, and best reserved for special occasions. It's not the everyday workhorse of your kitchen, but when you want to add a touch of sophistication, it's the oil to reach for. Just don't expect it to play well with your bhindi masala or aloo gobi. Olive oil has its place, and when used thoughtfully, it can bring a little Mediterranean flair to even the most spice-laden kitchens.

Avocado Oil: Fancy, Fat, and Expensive

Avocado oil is the oil equivalent of an Instagram influencer—always perfectly filtered, effortlessly chic, and slightly out of reach for most of us. It's marketed as the ultimate in health and luxury, promising everything from glowing skin to heart health. But for all its hype, does it deserve a permanent spot in your kitchen, or is it just the avocado toast of oils—overpriced and overhyped?

Let's start with the basics. Avocado oil is extracted from the pulp of avocados, not the seed, which gives it a buttery texture and mild, slightly nutty flavour. Unlike many oils that require heavy processing, good-quality avocado oil is cold-pressed, retaining most of its nutrients and that lovely green hue. It's packed with monounsaturated fats, antioxidants, and vitamin E, making it a darling of nutritionists and beauty gurus alike.

The health benefits of avocado oil are indeed impressive. Its monounsaturated fats are the same heart-healthy fats found in olive oil, helping to reduce bad cholesterol and increase good cholesterol. It's also a rich source of lutein, an antioxidant that supports eye health, and vitamin E, which is great for your skin. Avocado oil's anti-inflammatory properties make it a favourite among those with joint pain or autoimmune conditions. It's like a multivitamin in liquid form, except it tastes way better.

Where avocado oil really shines, though, is its smoke point. At a whopping 270°C, it's one of the highest smoke points of any cooking oil, meaning it's practically unbreakable under heat. This makes it perfect for high-heat cooking methods like frying, roasting, and searing. Unlike extra-virgin olive oil, which throws a tantrum the moment the heat goes up, avocado oil stays calm and composed, preserving its nutrients and flavour.

But here's the catch: avocado oil isn't cheap. A single bottle can cost more than your entire spice collection, making it a luxury item for most kitchens. And while it's undeniably versatile, you have to wonder if it's really worth using to fry up some aloo tikki or drizzle over your dal. For everyday cooking, the price-to-benefit ratio might not work for everyone, especially when there are more affordable options like ghee or mustard oil.

Another thing to consider is flavour. Avocado oil has a mild, neutral taste that works beautifully in certain dishes but doesn't bring much character to the table. For recipes that rely on the oil to add depth, like a mustard oil-laced achaar or a ghee-laden halwa, avocado oil feels like a dull understudy stepping into a leading role. It's great for when you don't want the oil to steal the spotlight, like in stir-fries or baked dishes, but it won't win any awards for flavour.

So where does avocado oil belong in the Indian kitchen? For one, it's a fantastic choice for those who love experimenting with global cuisines. If you're into making guacamole, roasting vegetables, or whipping up salad dressings, avocado oil is a dream. Its creamy texture and high smoke point also make it ideal for grilling or pan-searing meats and fish, giving them a golden, crispy exterior without any of the burned aftertaste that comes with lower-smoke-point oils.

In terms of Indian dishes, avocado oil works best in recipes that don't require high levels of spice or long cooking times. Use it for stir-fried veggies, light curries, or even as a substitute for butter in baking. Its health benefits also make it a good choice for those with dietary restrictions or anyone looking to reduce their intake of saturated fats. But let's be honest—if you're frying up pakoras or making a rich biryani, you'll probably reach for ghee before avocado oil.

There's also the sustainability angle to consider. Avocado oil is made from avocados (obviously), and avocados are notorious for their environmental footprint. They require a lot of water to grow, and the global demand for avocados has led to deforestation and unsustainable farming practices in some regions. While buying organic or fair-trade avocado oil can help mitigate these issues, it's worth thinking about whether the health benefits are worth the environmental cost.

For those who can afford it, avocado oil can be a wonderful addition to the kitchen. It's versatile, nutrient-rich, and performs beautifully under heat. But it's not a one-size-fits-all solution, and its price tag means it's unlikely to become a staple in most Indian households. Instead, think of it as a specialty oil, one that's great for specific uses but doesn't need to replace your everyday cooking fats.

The best way to use avocado oil is to play to its strengths. Use it where its high smoke point and neutral flavour can shine—like frying up an egg, roasting vegetables, or making a vinaigrette. For dishes that demand bold, robust Flavors, stick to traditional oils like mustard, coconut, or ghee. Avocado oil is like the minimalist friend who wears nothing but beige—it's stylish and dependable, but sometimes you just want someone who can rock a bright yellow sari.

At the end of the day, avocado oil is a bit of a show-off, but it's a show-off with substance. If you can afford to keep a bottle on hand, it's worth exploring its potential. Just don't let its Instagram-perfect image fool you into thinking it's a must-have for every meal. Like the avocado toast it's often paired with, it's a luxury, not a necessity—but sometimes, a little luxury is exactly what your kitchen needs.

Rice Bran Oil: The Quiet Overachiever

If cooking oils were people, rice bran oil would be that reliable friend who always has your back but never demands the spotlight. It's not as flashy as avocado oil, nor does it carry the cultural legacy of ghee or mustard oil. Yet, rice bran oil has quietly climbed its way into Indian kitchens, becoming a go-to option for everything from frying puris to stir-frying vegetables. With its high smoke point, neutral flavour, and "heart-healthy" reputation, it's no wonder rice bran oil is earning its stripes.

Rice bran oil is extracted from the outer layer of rice grains—the bran—which is typically a byproduct of rice milling. What's remarkable is how much goodness is packed into that humble layer. This oil is rich in vitamin E, antioxidants like gamma oryzanol, and a balanced mix of monounsaturated and polyunsaturated fats. If oils had resumes, rice bran oils would look like a LinkedIn profile designed to make you feel inadequate.

One of rice bran oil's biggest selling points is its smoke point. At 232°C, it's as heat-resistant as they come, making it ideal for deep-frying and high-heat cooking. It's the oil equivalent of someone who stays cool under pressure, refusing to crack even when the heat is on. Whether you're frying up samosas or making a spicy stir-fry, rice bran oil performs like a champ, maintaining its stability and keeping your kitchen smoke-free.

The neutral flavour is another tick in its favour. Unlike mustard oil, which announces its presence with a punchy, peppery aroma, or coconut oil, which brings its own tropical vibe, rice bran oil is a wallflower. It doesn't try to upstage the spices or overshadow the dish. Instead, it lets the other ingredients take centre stage, blending seamlessly into everything from curries to desserts. If you've ever felt like your oil was stealing the show, rice bran oil is the antidote.

But is it as healthy as the marketing suggests? Let's dive into the science. The presence of gamma oryzanol, a unique antioxidant compound, gives rice bran oil its "heart-healthy" reputation. Studies suggest that gamma oryzanol can help reduce bad cholesterol (LDL) while boosting good cholesterol (HDL), making it a favourite among cardiologists. Add to that the natural vitamin E content, which supports skin health and immune function, and you've got an oil that's not just functional but genuinely beneficial.

However, there's a catch—omega-6 fatty acids. Like many vegetable oils, rice bran oil is relatively high in omega-6 fats, which can be problematic if consumed in excess. While omega-6 is an essential fatty acid that the body needs, too much of it can lead to an imbalance with omega-3s, potentially causing inflammation. Given that the average Indian diet already leans heavily on omega-6-rich oils, it's worth using rice bran oil in moderation and balancing it with omega-3 sources like flaxseeds or fatty fish.

Another point to consider is that rice bran oil is refined, which means it undergoes processing to remove impurities. While this gives it its long shelf life and neutral taste, it also strips away some of the natural nutrients found in unrefined oils. The refining process isn't inherently bad—after all, it's what makes rice bran oil so versatile— but it's a reminder to rotate it with cold-pressed or less processed oils for a more nutrient-dense diet.

In terms of sustainability, rice bran oil scores surprisingly high. Since it's derived from a byproduct of rice production, it's essentially making use of what would otherwise go to waste. This makes it a more environmentally friendly choice compared to oils like avocado or palm oil, which can have significant ecological footprints.

Choosing rice bran oil feels less like contributing to deforestation and more like giving a humble grain it's time to shine.

So, where does rice bran oil fit into the Indian kitchen? Pretty much anywhere you need it to. Its high smoke point makes it perfect for deep-frying pakoras, puris, or jalebis. The neutral flavour means it won't clash with masalas or overshadow delicate Flavors, making it a solid choice for stir-fries, pulaos, or even baking. It's also an excellent backup oil—when you're running low on ghee or coconut oil, rice bran oil steps in without fuss or fanfare.

But is it exciting? Not really. Rice bran oil is more like the reliable workhorse of oils than the star attraction. It won't make you swoon like the aroma of mustard oil heating up or the richness of ghee melting in a pan. However, its versatility, health benefits, and ability to handle high heat make it an indispensable part of any modern kitchen. Think of it as the oil equivalent of a dependable pair of sneakers: not glamorous, but essential.

In a world where cooking oils often come with bold claims and hefty price tags, rice bran oil keeps things refreshingly simple. It doesn't promise miracles or try to reinvent the wheel. Instead, it delivers steady performance, balanced nutrition, and an ease of use that makes it a favourite for both seasoned cooks and beginners. So, while it may not have the flashiness of extra-virgin olive oil or the legacy of mustard oil, rice bran oil quietly holds its ground as one of the most versatile and reliable options out there.

The Great Match – Oils for Every Dish

Cooking is an art, and oils are the paints. But not all paints are created equal, and neither are oils. The key to elevating your dishes lies in pairing the right oil with the right cooking method. You wouldn't deep-fry samosas in olive oil any more than you'd sketch the Mona Lisa with a highlighter. Each oil has a personality, a smoke point, and a flavour profile that makes it suited—or completely unsuited—for certain dishes. Let's unravel the great mystery of matching oils to your recipes, so your kitchen adventures go off without a hitch.

For starters, there's deep-frying—the glorious, indulgent art of making crispy pakoras, flaky samosas, and golden jalebis. High heat is the name of the game here, which means you need oils that can handle temperatures around 180–200°C without breaking a sweat—or worse, breaking down. Ghee, with its rich aroma and buttery taste, is the reigning champion of deep-frying. It not only tolerates high heat like a boss but also imparts an unparalleled depth of flavour. For a lighter option, mustard oil is another strong contender, especially if you're going for North Indian or Bengali dishes where its peppery punch complements the spices. If you're looking for something more neutral, rice bran oil steps up as the workhorse of deep-frying. Its high smoke point and subtle flavour ensure that the crispy exterior of your puris or pakoras takes centre stage.

Now, let's talk stir-frying and searing, the quick-draw cooking methods that demand oils capable of standing up to moderately high heat without losing their cool—or their nutrients. This is where oils like peanut oil and refined olive oil come into play. Peanut oil, with its subtle nutty undertones, is perfect for stir-frying vegetables, meats, or even noodles. It has a high smoke point and adds just enough character to the dish without overpowering the spices. Refined olive oil, while not as glamorous as its extra-virgin sibling, is well-suited for sautéing and searing, especially when you're going for a Mediterranean-Indian fusion vibe. Imagine a plate of sautéed veggies kissed with a touch of olive oil and a sprinkle of cumin seeds—it's a match made in culinary heaven.

But not all cooking is about high drama and sizzling pans. Some dishes demand a gentler touch, like tempering spices for a fragrant dal or slowly caramelizing onions for a rich curry base. Enter coconut oil and ghee, the power couple of medium-heat cooking. Coconut oil, with its sweet, tropical aroma, is a must for South Indian tempering. It plays beautifully with curry leaves, mustard seeds, and dried red chilies, adding a signature fragrance that transports you straight to Kerala. Ghee, on the other hand, is the MVP of slow-cooking and tempering across cuisines. It doesn't just carry Flavors; it amplifies them, making every spice in your tadka sing in harmony.

And then there's drizzling and finishing, the final flourish that elevates a dish from good to unforgettable. Oils used in this context aren't just about function; they're about flair. Extra-virgin olive oil, with its grassy aroma and fruity notes, is the undisputed king of finishing oils. While it's out of its depth in a hot tadka pan, a drizzle over roasted vegetables, fresh salads, or even a bowl of hummus is like adding the perfect accessory to an outfit. Sesame oil, too, shines in this role. Its toasty, nutty flavour is a game-changer in Asian-inspired dishes, whether drizzled over noodles or added to a dipping sauce. Flaxseed oil, though less common, is another worthy contender. Its earthy taste pairs beautifully with cold dishes and even smoothies, offering a nutritional boost along with its subtle flavour.

But here's where things get tricky. Choosing the right oil isn't just about taste or cooking method; it's also about balancing health considerations. For example, while sunflower oil is a popular choice in many Indian households, its high omega-6 content means it's best used sparingly. Similarly, while coconut oil is a dream for frying and tempering, its saturated fat content makes moderation key. The same goes for olive oil; while extra-virgin is great for drizzling, refined olive oil is better for medium-heat cooking. The goal is to rotate oils, mixing and matching based on the dish, the cooking method, and your health priorities.

Then there's the question of blending tradition with modern trends. Ghee and mustard oil are steeped in history, with roots in Ayurvedic practices and regional cuisines, while oils like avocado and rice bran are relative newcomers, riding the wave of global health trends. The beauty of Indian cooking is its adaptability, so why not embrace both? Use ghee for a rich tadka, olive oil for a fresh salad, and avocado oil for stir-frying—all in one week. It's not about picking sides; it's about playing to each oil's strengths.

Storage is another critical piece of the puzzle. Oils, especially unrefined ones, are prone to oxidation, which can lead to rancidity and the formation of harmful compounds. Store oils in cool, dark places, and keep the caps tightly sealed to maintain freshness. For cold-pressed oils, consider refrigeration to extend their shelf life. And always give your oils a sniff test before using—if it smells off, it's time to toss it.

Finally, let's debunk a myth or two. No, mixing oils doesn't cancel out their health benefits, so feel free to combine ghee and mustard oil for a unique frying blend. And no, you don't need to splurge on every fancy oil that hits the market. Stick to a core lineup that suits your cooking style, and add specialty oils as your culinary adventures expand.

At the end of the day, cooking is as much about intuition as it is about technique. Trust your taste buds, understand your ingredients, and let the oils you choose reflect the dish you're creating. With the right oils in your arsenal, every meal can be a masterpiece, whether it's a humble dal or a lavish biryani. So go ahead—pour, sizzle, and drizzle your way to deliciousness.

Balancing Health, Flavour, and Your Wallet

Cooking oils sit at the intersection of health, flavour, and finance, creating a culinary Rubik's cube we're all trying to solve. On one end, you've got premium, cold-pressed oils promising better health and flavour at prices that could finance a small vacation. On the other end, there's the wallet-friendly, refined stuff that's as stripped of nutrients as it is personality. Somewhere in between lies the art of balancing these competing factors without sacrificing your taste buds—or your monthly budget. Let's dive into how you can make smart oil choices that keep your meals flavourful, your body healthy, and your wallet intact.

First things first: the question of cost. Premium oils like extra-virgin olive oil, avocado oil, or cold-pressed mustard oil can feel like a splurge, especially when you see cheaper refined oils sitting right next to them on the supermarket shelf. But before you reach for the bargain bottle, consider this: while high-quality oils cost more upfront, they often deliver more in terms of both flavour and health. A little drizzle of extra-virgin olive oil on your salad can do more for your palate than a tablespoon of generic vegetable oil ever could. Similarly, cold-pressed oils pack a nutritional punch that refined oils can't match, so you end up using less while reaping more benefits.

But does this mean you need to banish all refined oils from your kitchen? Not necessarily. Refined oils have their place, especially when you're cooking in bulk or for high-heat methods like deep-frying. Frying up a batch of samosas in cold-pressed avocado oil might sound virtuous, but it's also wildly impractical—and unnecessary. For such occasions, a neutral oil like refined sunflower or rice bran can get the job done without breaking the bank. The trick is to reserve your premium oils for dishes where their flavour and nutritional qualities can shine, like finishing salads or drizzling over roasted vegetables.

Storage is another area where health and cost intersect. Oils, particularly unrefined ones, are prone to oxidation, which not only diminishes their flavour but can also generate harmful compounds. Proper storage can extend the life of your oils, ensuring you get your money's worth. Keep your oils in cool, dark places, and consider using smaller bottles for specialty oils to avoid wastage. Refrigeration is a good option for oils like flaxseed or walnut, which are especially prone to rancidity. And remember, even the best oils won't save a dish if they've gone off, so don't hesitate to toss anything that smells funky.

Now let's talk about health. With so much noise around "good" and "bad" fats, it's easy to get overwhelmed—or worse, fall for the latest health craze. The reality is that no single oil can be your one-stop solution. A balanced diet requires a mix of fats, from the monounsaturated magic of olive oil to the saturated strength of coconut oil. The key is moderation and variety. Rotate your oils like you would your spices, ensuring you're getting a range of nutrients without overloading on any one type of fat.

This brings us to the omega conundrum—specifically, the balance between omega-3 and omega-6 fatty acids. Modern diets, including many Indian ones, are disproportionately high in omega-6 thanks to the prevalence of refined vegetable oils. While omega-6 isn't inherently bad, an excess can tip the scales toward inflammation, which is linked to a host of chronic conditions. To counterbalance this, try incorporating more omega-3-rich oils like flaxseed or walnut into your diet, and pair them with fatty fish, nuts, and seeds for an extra boost. Even better, limit your reliance on omega-6-heavy oils like sunflower or soybean in favour of more balanced options like rice bran or mustard oil.

But what about flavour? After all, even the healthiest oil won't cut it if it leaves your dishes tasting flat. This is where the idea of "specialty oils" comes into play. Ghee, with its nutty richness, can elevate a humble dal to a restaurant-quality dish. Coconut oil adds a sweet, tropical depth to South Indian curries that no other fat can replicate. And let's not forget sesame oil, whose toasted aroma can turn a simple stir-fry into a masterpiece. These oils might not be your everyday go-to, but they're worth keeping on hand for those moments when flavour takes centre stage.

Of course, the ultimate balancing act is ensuring you're not just eating for pleasure or health, but also for practicality. One way to do this is by adopting a tiered approach to oils. Keep a high-smoke-point, neutral oil like rice bran or peanut for frying and bulk cooking. Use a mid-range, flavour-forward oil like mustard or sesame for tempering and everyday sautéing. And reserve the pricey stuff—your cold-pressed coconut or extra-virgin olive—for finishing touches and low-heat dishes. This way, you're not just rotating oils for health; you're also maximizing their culinary potential.

And let's not forget sustainability—a topic that's increasingly important as we become more conscious of our environmental footprint. Many premium oils come with certifications for organic farming, fair trade, or sustainable production. While these labels often come with a higher price tag, they reflect a commitment to ethical and environmentally friendly practices. If this aligns with your values, consider supporting brands that prioritize sustainability, knowing your investment benefits more than just your health.

Finally, there's the matter of waste—or more specifically, avoiding it. Oils are perishable, and buying in bulk might seem economical, but it's a false economy if half of it goes rancid before you can use it. Instead, buy smaller quantities of premium oils and rotate them regularly. For high-use oils, like those for frying, opt for larger bottles but decant into smaller, easy-to-use containers. This not only preserves freshness but also makes you more mindful of how much you're using—a win for both health and budget.

In the end, balancing health, flavour, and finances isn't about finding the perfect oil—it's about making smarter, more intentional choices. With a little planning and creativity, you can create a kitchen that caters to your taste buds, supports your well-being, and keeps your wallet happy. So, stock up wisely, store thoughtfully, and cook with confidence, knowing that every drop of oil is working its magic.

PART II

Reclaiming Your Kitchen

Chapter 4

Nostalgic Carbs – Making Classics Like Pasta, Paneer, and Parathas Healthier

The Love Affair with Carbs

Carbs are like that charismatic friend who lights up the room—impossible to ignore, deeply comforting, and occasionally misunderstood. Think of the joy in biting into a hot, flaky paratha fresh off the tawa or the irresistible pull of a plate of pasta twirled to perfection. From fragrant pulao to soft, buttery naan, carbs have been our go-to comfort food for centuries. They're not just staples; they're emotional anchors, cultural symbols, and, frankly, the heart of any good meal.

But somewhere along the way, carbs fell from grace. As diet trends exploded and social media influencers took over, carbs found themselves painted as villains. The message was clear: if you wanted a flat stomach or endless energy, carbs had to go. We were told to swap our rotis for lettuce wraps, our rice for quinoa, and our beloved bread for cauliflower-based everything. Sure, cauliflower is versatile, but cauliflower "bread"? Let's not lie to ourselves.

Cutting carbs became the new badge of honour in the diet world. Yet, if you've ever tried to kick them to the curb, you know how miserable life without carbs can be. Day one: optimism. Day two: irritability. Day three: fantasizing about pasta and wondering if cauliflower can file for emotional damages. By the end of week one, you're binging on whatever carb-laden treat you can find, realizing carbs weren't the problem—it was your unrealistic expectations.

The truth is, carbs aren't the dietary villains they're made out to be. They're essential for energy, brain function, and overall health. What matters is the type of carbs you choose and how you incorporate them into your meals. Refined carbs—like white bread, sugary snacks, and ultra-processed foods—can cause blood sugar spikes and offer little nutritional value. But whole carbs? That's where the magic happens. Think brown rice, oats, whole-grain bread, and millets. These are packed with fiber, vitamins, and slow-releasing energy, making them a nutritional powerhouse.

Culturally, carbs are the backbone of most traditional cuisines, especially in India. Picture a thali without rice or roti. Impossible, right? Across the world, carbs tell a story: the Italians have their al dente pasta, the French their artisanal bread, and Indians their never-ending love affair with parathas, dosas, and biryanis. These aren't just dishes—they're edible love letters to our heritage. A Sunday lunch with steaming pulao and raita, or a breakfast of crispy aloo parathas with pickle, evokes memories of family gatherings and kitchen conversations.

The anti-carb movement, while well-intentioned, forgot to account for this emotional and cultural connection. It's easy to vilify food when you strip it of its context. But carbs aren't just food; they're part of who we are. They fuel marathon runners and busy moms. They're what we crave after a hard day. They're how many of us connect with our heritage, offering a taste of home no matter where we are.

So, why do carbs get such a bad rap? Blame it on processed foods and oversized portions. When we load up on highly refined carbs like white bread, pastries, and sugar-laden snacks, we miss out on fiber and nutrients while consuming empty calories. These foods digest quickly, causing blood sugar spikes and crashes that leave us hungry and sluggish. But when you switch to whole grains, legumes, and fiber-rich carb sources, you get steady energy, improved digestion, and a fuller, more satisfied belly.

Let's also talk about moderation, the unsung hero of healthy eating. Carbs, even the good ones, are best enjoyed in balanced portions. Pair them with proteins, healthy fats, and colourful vegetables to create meals that are as nourishing as they are delicious. A bowl of rice feels a lot less indulgent when it's served with a hearty dal, sautéed spinach, and a drizzle of ghee. And pasta, when combined with a veggie-packed tomato sauce or a sprinkle of lean protein, goes from guilty pleasure to balanced meal.

Of course, the joy of carbs lies not just in their nutritional value but in how they make us feel. There's nothing quite like the first bite of a warm paratha, dipped in tangy achar, or the satisfaction of swirling your fork through a plate of spaghetti Bolognese. These are the foods we celebrate with, the ones we turn to on tough days. They're comfort in its purest form.

As we navigate this carb-conscious world, it's worth remembering that it's not about deprivation; it's about choice. Swap refined carbs for whole grains, incorporate more fiber, and balance your plate with thoughtful pairings. Most importantly, stop demonizing carbs. They're not the enemy; they're a cherished part of life's table.

Carbs are more than just calories—they're culture, comfort, and a culinary hug. Cutting them out entirely isn't just impractical; it's unnecessary. With a little intention and a lot of love, you can savour every bite without guilt. Because life's too short to live without carbs—and let's face it, cauliflower will never come close to the joy of a hot, buttery naan.

Pasta with a Purpose

Pasta is comfort food in its purest form—a warm bowl of spaghetti, swirling strands of fettuccine, or tiny, joyful bites of penne all drenched in sauces that can be indulgent or simple. It's a love language, universally understood and endlessly versatile. But pasta's reputation as a carb-heavy indulgence has left many of us in a love-hate relationship with this Italian classic. After all, how do you justify a giant plate of carbonara when you're trying to "eat clean"?

The good news is, pasta doesn't have to be an all-or-nothing deal. You don't have to trade alfredo for sadness, nor spaghetti for spiralized zucchini every single time (though zucchini noodles are surprisingly delightful). By making a few smart choices—starting with the type of pasta you buy and the way you prepare it—you can transform pasta from a guilty pleasure into a nutrient-packed, flavourful meal.

Let's begin with the pasta aisle itself, which has undergone a transformation in recent years. Once, it was simple: spaghetti, penne, and maybe a box of lasagna sheets. Now, it's an overwhelming display of possibilities: whole-grain pasta, chickpea fusilli, lentil penne, and even quinoa spaghetti. Traditional pasta, made from refined wheat flour, is undeniably delicious but comes with fewer nutrients and a higher glycaemic index. This means it digests quickly, giving you a short-lived burst of energy followed by a carb crash.

Whole-grain pasta, on the other hand, retains the fiber-rich bran and germ of the wheat, which slows digestion, keeps you fuller for longer, and delivers essential nutrients like iron and B vitamins. Then there are the protein-packed options made from lentils, chickpeas, or even black beans. These are excellent for anyone looking to boost protein intake while keeping carbs in check. The best part? They have a hearty texture and nutty flavour that pairs beautifully with robust sauces.

Of course, there's always the low-carb "pasta" option—zoodles (zucchini noodles) and spaghetti squash. These vegetable-based alternatives are fantastic for light meals or when you want to pack in extra veggies. But let's be real: zoodles are not pasta. They're an entirely different experience, and Italians everywhere would weep at the thought of zucchini replacing their beloved spaghetti.

Speaking of Italians, they would probably faint at what we've done to their sauces. Creamy cauliflower alfredo, anyone? While it may sound sacrilegious to purists, adding vegetables to pasta sauces is a brilliant way to boost flavour, texture, and nutrients. For instance, blending roasted red peppers or butternut squash into a silky sauce gives you a creamy, satisfying texture without the heavy cream. Even traditional tomato sauces can benefit from the addition of carrots, spinach, or zucchini, which blend seamlessly while adding fiber and vitamins.

The key to making healthier pasta isn't just the type of pasta or sauce you choose—it's also the ratio of pasta to everything else on your plate. Instead of a heaping pile of spaghetti with a few scattered vegetables, flip the script. Aim for equal parts pasta, vegetables, and protein. This creates a balanced, satisfying meal that won't leave you reaching for snacks two hours later.

For example, a simple spaghetti aglio e olio (garlic and olive oil) can be transformed by tossing in sautéed spinach, roasted cherry tomatoes, and a handful of grilled shrimps. Or, take your classic mac and cheese: swap some of the pasta for steamed cauliflower, mix in a lighter cheese sauce made with Greek yogurt, and top with crunchy whole-grain breadcrumbs for a dish that feels decadent but packs a nutritional punch.

Let's not forget the power of portion control. Pasta dishes in restaurants often come in serving sizes that could feed a small village. At home, aim for about 2 ounces of dry pasta per person— that's roughly one cup cooked. Pair it with a generous helping of vegetables and a lean protein source, and you've got a satisfying, balanced plate.

One often-overlooked trick is to cook pasta al dente—just firm to the bite. Not only is this how it's traditionally served in Italy, but it also lowers the glycaemic index of the dish, preventing rapid blood sugar spikes. Plus, it tastes infinitely better than mushy, overcooked pasta, which has no place in anyone's kitchen.

Another secret weapon? Herbs and spices. Fresh basil, parsley, oregano, or even a sprinkle of red chili flakes can elevate a simple pasta dish without adding calories. And let's not underestimate the power of good olive oil. A small drizzle of high-quality olive oil, added at the end of cooking, can transform an ordinary dish into something extraordinary.

And now for the elephant in the room: cheese. What's pasta without a generous helping of Parmesan, mozzarella, or creamy ricotta? While cheese adds undeniable flavour and richness, it's easy to overdo. Instead of drowning your pasta in cheese, try using it sparingly as a finishing touch. A small grating of Parmesan over the top can deliver all the flavour you need without turning your plate into a calorie bomb. Or, experiment with nutritional yeast, a plant-based alternative that offers a cheesy flavour with none of the fat.

Let's also take a moment to acknowledge the joy of experimenting with global Flavors. Who says pasta has to be Italian? Thai-inspired peanut noodles, Indian-style masala macaroni, or a simple Mediterranean pasta salad with olives, feta, and roasted vegetables can bring exciting twists to your weekly meals. These variations not only keep things interesting but also allow you to incorporate different ingredients and Flavors into your diet.

Ultimately, pasta is what you make of it. It can be a vehicle for nutrient-dense meals or an indulgent treat, depending on how you prepare and serve it. The next time you're craving a bowl of pasta, don't reach for the guilt. Reach for the vegetables, the whole grains, and the olive oil. Play around with sauces, try new pasta varieties, and embrace the endless possibilities.

Because at the end of the day, pasta isn't just food—it's comfort, creativity, and a celebration of culinary joy. And with a few thoughtful tweaks, you can enjoy it without a single ounce of regret.

Paneer, but Smarter

Paneer, the king of Indian vegetarian cuisine, is as versatile as it is beloved. From luscious gravies to smoky tikka skewers, paneer makes its way onto plates across the country in forms that range from indulgent to ingenious. But let's face it: as delicious as paneer is, it's also a calorie bomb when deep-fried, smothered in cream, or paired with buttery naan. The good news? You don't have to swear off paneer to maintain a balanced diet. With a few clever tweaks, you can have your paneer and eat it too—without guilt or grease stains on your conscience.

First, let's talk about the star ingredient itself. Paneer, for all its decadence, is essentially a block of fresh cheese made by curdling milk. Its appeal lies in its mild flavour, which soaks up spices like a dream, and its creamy texture, which pairs beautifully with just about anything. It's also packed with protein and calcium, making it a fantastic choice for vegetarians who need a hearty, satisfying ingredient. The catch? Paneer is relatively high in fat, especially if it's made from full-cream milk.

Enter the low-fat paneer revolution. By making paneer at home using skim milk or low-fat milk, you can significantly cut down on its calorie content without compromising on taste. All you need is milk, a bit of lemon juice or vinegar, and a willingness to stir. The result? A lighter, healthier version of your favourite ingredient that still delivers on creaminess.

But what if you're looking for an even lighter alternative? Enter tofu, paneer's protein-packed cousin. Made from soy milk, tofu has a similar texture to paneer and can be used in nearly all the same ways. It's lower in calories and fat, making it ideal for those days when you want a leaner protein source. Plus, tofu absorbs marinades and spices just as well, whether you're grilling, baking, or stir-frying it. While it may not have the rich dairy flavour of paneer, it brings its own nutty, mild taste to the table—a small trade-off for a lighter plate.

Once you've got your paneer (or tofu) ready, the next question is how to cook it. Traditional methods often involve frying, which, while delicious, adds unnecessary fat. Grilling or baking paneer is a game-changer. Marinate the cubes in a mixture of yogurt, lemon juice, and spices like cumin, turmeric, and garam masala, then thread them onto skewers and grill until golden and slightly charred. The result? Smoky, flavourful bites that are perfect for salads, wraps, or a protein-packed snack.

If you're craving a rich curry, you can still indulge without turning your kitchen into a cream factory. The secret lies in substituting heavy cream with lighter alternatives. Greek yogurt, for instance, is a fantastic stand-in for cream in recipes like paneer makhani or butter paneer. It adds tanginess and richness while cutting down on calories. Another trick? Blending soaked cashews with a splash of water to create a creamy, dairy-free base for your gravies. This not only lightens the dish but also adds a subtle nutty flavour that enhances the spices.

For those days when you're feeling adventurous, why not let paneer star in some creative new recipes? Think beyond the usual suspects like palak paneer or shahi paneer. Paneer tikka salad, for example, is a refreshing twist on the classic appetizer. Combine grilled paneer tikka with crunchy greens, cucumber, cherry tomatoes, and a light lemon-yogurt dressing for a dish that's as satisfying as it is nutritious. Or try paneer-stuffed bell peppers: hollow out colourful bell peppers, fill them with a mixture of crumbled paneer, vegetables, and spices, and bake until tender. It's a fun, high-protein meal that looks as good as it tastes.

And let's not forget paneer wraps, the ultimate on-the-go meal. Swap out fried fillings for grilled paneer strips, wrap them in a whole-grain roti with fresh vegetables and a dollop of mint chutney, and voilà—a lunch that's hearty, wholesome, and deliciously portable.

While we're reinventing paneer, let's also address the elephant in the room: portion control. Paneer is rich and filling, which means you don't need a giant block of it to satisfy your cravings. By pairing it with fiber-rich vegetables, lentils, or whole grains, you can create a balanced meal that doesn't overload on calories. For example, instead of a giant bowl of butter paneer with naan, try a smaller portion served with brown rice and a side of roasted vegetables. This way, you get the creaminess of paneer without skimping on nutrients.

Speaking of vegetables, paneer and greens are a match made in culinary heaven. Palak paneer, the classic spinach and paneer dish, is a great example of how to balance protein with nutrient-dense vegetables. But why stop at spinach? Methi paneer (with fenugreek leaves), saag paneer (with mustard greens), or even kale paneer (for those feeling adventurous) are equally delicious options. The greens not only add vitamins and minerals but also help balance the richness of the paneer.

For those who insist on a little indulgence, there's always the option to compromise. Fry your paneer, but sparingly—perhaps just a light pan-fry in minimal oil for that golden crust. Or use a non-stick pan to achieve a similar effect without the extra calories. And if you can't resist a creamy sauce, go ahead—just keep your portions reasonable and balance the rest of the meal with lighter sides.

At the end of the day, paneer isn't the problem—it's how we cook and pair it. By making small, thoughtful changes, you can enjoy all the cheesy goodness without turning every meal into a calorie extravaganza. Whether you're grilling it, stuffing it into wraps, or letting it shine in a veggie-packed curry, paneer can be as healthy as you want it to be.

So go ahead, embrace your love for paneer. Experiment with lighter preparations, try new pairings, and rediscover why this humble block of cheese has earned its place as a culinary icon. After all, life's too short to live without paneer—especially when it can be this good for you.

Parathas That Don't Break Your Diet

Ah, parathas—the ultimate comfort food. Whether stuffed with spiced potatoes, paneer, or simply slathered in butter, these flaky, golden flatbreads have a way of winning hearts and obliterating diets. But who says parathas can't be indulgent and healthy at the same time? With a little creativity and some smart swaps, you can enjoy this beloved dish without sabotaging your health goals. Let's take a deep dive into how to make parathas that are every bit as delicious as the ones from your childhood, but with a modern, nutritious twist.

Let's start with the dough, the backbone of any good paratha. Most traditional recipes call for all-purpose flour (maida) or whole wheat flour (atta). While whole wheat flour is a better choice nutritionally, why stop there? You can boost the fiber and nutrient content of your dough by mixing in whole-grain flours like ragi (finger millet), bajra (pearl millet), or jowar (sorghum). These ancient grains are rich in iron, calcium, and fiber, making your parathas more filling and better for digestion.

For an extra dose of health, consider adding seeds or leafy greens to the dough. Flaxseeds, chia seeds, or sesame seeds not only add texture but also bring omega-3 fatty acids and antioxidants to the party. As for greens, finely chopped spinach, methi (fenugreek leaves), or coriander leaves can be kneaded directly into the dough, giving your parathas a vibrant green hue and an earthy flavour that's impossible to resist.

Now, let's talk stuffing. Traditional fillings like aloo (potato) or paneer are delicious, but they can be heavy on carbs or fats when overdone. The trick is to bulk up your stuffing with nutrient-dense ingredients. For example, in an aloo paratha, mix boiled potatoes with grated carrots, steamed broccoli, or even green peas. Not only do these veggies add vitamins and fiber, but they also enhance the flavour and texture of the stuffing. For paneer parathas, try combining crumbled paneer with finely chopped spinach, methi, or grated zucchini for a lighter, protein-packed filling.

If you're feeling adventurous, break away from the classics and experiment with less conventional stuffings. Think roasted sweet potato and quinoa, mashed chickpeas with spices, or even a mix of grated beetroot and carrots. These combinations bring a fresh twist to your parathas while keeping them nutrient-dense and satisfying.

Of course, the real challenge with parathas is cooking them without drowning them in ghee or oil. Don't get me wrong—there's nothing quite like the taste of a paratha cooked in butter, but if you're watching your fat intake, there are plenty of alternatives. For starters, consider using a non-stick or cast-iron pan. These pans require far less oil and still give you that beautiful golden-brown finish.

When it comes to the cooking fat itself, think quality over quantity. Instead of slathering on ghee, try brushing a thin layer over each side of the paratha. This technique lets you retain the rich, buttery flavour with a fraction of the calories. Alternatively, use heart-healthy oils like avocado or olive oil in small amounts. And if you're feeling particularly virtuous, skip the fat altogether and dry-roast your parathas—you'll be surprised at how good they taste even without the grease.

For those who've embraced the air fryer revolution, parathas adapt beautifully to this gadget. Brush your parathas lightly with oil and pop them into the air fryer for a few minutes. The result? Crispy, golden parathas that taste indulgent but are significantly lighter than their pan-fried counterparts. Sure, it's not "traditional," but when has innovation ever hurt anyone?

And let's not overlook the role of spices and herbs in making your parathas healthier and more flavourful. Adding ajwain (carom seeds) or cumin seeds to the dough not only enhances the taste but also aids digestion. A sprinkle of black pepper, turmeric, or chili flakes in your stuffing can bring a kick of flavour and a boost of antioxidants. The best part? These small additions take your parathas from good to unforgettable without adding any calories.

Another aspect to consider is portion control. Parathas are so delicious that it's easy to lose track of how many you've devoured. A simple way to manage portions is by rolling out slightly smaller parathas and pairing them with nutrient-dense sides. Instead of serving parathas with a heavy curry, try lighter accompaniments like a refreshing cucumber-yogurt raita, a tangy mint chutney, or a colourful salad of tomatoes, onions, and fresh herbs. These sides not only balance the richness of the parathas but also make the meal feel more complete and satisfying.

And for those with a sweet tooth, don't think parathas are off-limits. Sweet parathas, like those stuffed with jaggery or dates, can be made healthier by using whole wheat flour and reducing the sugar content. For an even lighter option, try spreading a thin layer of almond or peanut butter on a warm paratha and sprinkling it with cinnamon—it's like a healthy dessert disguised as breakfast.

What about freezing parathas for those busy mornings? Absolutely! Homemade frozen parathas are a lifesaver and far healthier than store-bought ones. Simply roll out your parathas, layer them between sheets of parchment paper, and freeze. When you're ready to cook, take one out and toss it straight onto a hot pan—no defrosting required. This way, you always have a healthier option on hand, no matter how hectic life gets.

At its core, the paratha is a humble dish—simple, versatile, and deeply satisfying. By making a few thoughtful changes, you can elevate it into something that's not just delicious but also nourishing. Whether you're mixing superfoods into the dough, experimenting with creative fillings, or finding new ways to cook them, the possibilities are endless.

So go ahead, roll out that dough, fire up the pan (or air fryer), and rediscover why parathas hold such a special place in our hearts. With these tweaks, you'll find that it's possible to enjoy every flaky, buttery bite without any of the guilt. After all, life's too short for boring breakfasts—or boring parathas.

Chapter 5

Food Fads & Fibs – Debunking Ridiculous Health Claims

The Buzzword Trap

Every aisle of the supermarket feels like a battle of wits. Boxes, bottles, and bags scream out promises that range from "gluten-free" to "detoxifying" to "superfood-powered," making you wonder if you've stumbled into a health food convention instead of your local store. These buzzwords prey on our desire to eat better, live longer, and feel good about our choices, but they're often smoke, and mirrors designed to make us spend more without actually improving our diets.

Let's start with the ultimate overachiever of health marketing: "superfoods." The term has no scientific basis, yet it conjures images of cape-wearing blueberries swooping in to rescue you from poor health. From chia seeds to acai berries, marketers have managed to take ordinary nutritious foods and turn them into high-priced, mystical elixirs. While chia seeds are undeniably rich in fiber and omega-3s, they aren't magical. Want the same benefits? Flaxseeds, grown right here in India, offer comparable nutrition at a fraction of the cost. And acai? Sure, it's packed with antioxidants, but so is the humble amla, the Indian gooseberry that's been boosting immunity long before the term "antioxidant" was coined.

Then there's "detox," perhaps the most overused and underexplained buzzword in the food industry. Detox teas, juices, and powders promise to flush out toxins as if your body's natural detox systems (hello, liver and kidneys) are on permanent vacation. Science tells us that unless you've been exposed to poison or extreme pollution, your organs do a fantastic job of detoxifying all on their own. Those $50 detox teas? They're likely just overpriced laxatives that leave you dehydrated and cranky. As for juice cleanses, let's just say I've been there, done that, and spent three days fantasizing about solid food.

The gluten-free craze is another masterclass in marketing. For people with celiac disease or gluten sensitivity, avoiding gluten is crucial. But for the rest of us, gluten-free doesn't necessarily mean healthier—it often just means pricier. Take gluten-free cookies, for instance: they're often loaded with sugar and fat to compensate for the lack of wheat. So unless you have a genuine intolerance, there's no need to fear that loaf of sourdough. In fact, whole-grain breads can be excellent sources of fiber and nutrients, unlike many gluten-free options, which are heavily processed.

"Organic" is another term that sounds wholesome but doesn't always deliver. Organic farming avoids synthetic pesticides and fertilizers, which is undoubtedly better for the environment, but an organic cookie is still…a cookie. The sugar and fat content don't magically disappear because the wheat was grown without chemicals. Similarly, "natural" is one of the most misleading labels out there. While it implies unprocessed and pure, the term is unregulated. A product can be labelled "natural" and still contain high-fructose corn syrup, preservatives, and a long list of unpronounceable additives.

And then there's the marketing genius behind "no added sugar." It makes you feel virtuous about choosing a product, but it doesn't mean it's sugar-free. It often means the sugar is naturally occurring, like in dates or fruit juice concentrate, which can still spike your blood sugar. Worse, some products compensate by adding artificial sweeteners, which come with their own set of health concerns.

Even "low-fat" and "fat-free" can be traps. When manufacturers remove fat from foods, they often add sugar, salt, or other fillers to make up for the lost flavour. That "fat-free" yogurt might have less fat but could contain more sugar than a candy bar. Similarly, foods labelled as "low-carb" are often full of unhealthy fats to make them palatable. You're better off eating balanced meals with whole ingredients than falling for these gimmicks.

Why do we fall for these traps? Because these buzzwords speak directly to our insecurities. Want to feel like you're eating clean? "Detox" it is. Want to avoid guilt while snacking? "Low-fat" to the rescue. Need to justify an expensive indulgence? Slap a "superfood" label on it, and suddenly, it's an investment in your health. Marketers know that we crave quick fixes, and they exploit that desire at every turn.

Of course, I'm no saint. There was a time I was convinced kale could solve all my problems. Kale chips, kale smoothies, kale on pizza—you name it, I tried it. Eventually, I realized that while kale is a great source of nutrients, it's not going to single-handedly transform my health. Similarly, I once bought into the detox tea craze, only to spend an entire weekend with nothing to show for it but frequent trips to the bathroom and an empty wallet.

The truth is, eating well doesn't require buzzwords or miracle foods. It's about balance, variety, and making informed choices. Instead of chasing the latest health trend, focus on incorporating nutrient-dense whole foods that don't rely on flashy labels to prove their worth. Trust me, your body—and your bank account—will thank you.

Ridiculous Diets, Debunked

If there's one thing the diet industry thrives on, it's our collective impatience. We want fast results, whether it's shedding pounds, glowing skin, or a metabolism that hums like a finely tuned Ferrari. Enter the parade of trendy diets, each claiming to be the one true path to health and happiness. Keto, Paleo, Juice Cleanses—they all have their moments in the sun, promising miraculous transformations and often leaving behind confusion, frustration, and an extra dose of cynicism. Let's unravel some of the madness, shall we?

The Keto Craze

Ah, keto: the diet that lets you eat butter-drenched bacon but scolds you for daring to look at a slice of bread. The ketogenic diet has surged in popularity for its ability to burn fat by putting your body into ketosis, a metabolic state where fat is used for fuel instead of carbohydrates. Sounds great, right? Except ketosis is as tricky to maintain as a long-distance relationship with someone who's bad at texting.

Sure, keto works—for a while. But have you tried going to an Indian wedding on keto? Forget samosas and gulab jamun; even the paneer gravy is laced with carbs. Plus, the so-called "keto flu," where your body protests the sudden lack of carbs with headaches and fatigue, is enough to make you question your life choices. Let's not forget your uncle who swears by keto but sneaks in parathas at breakfast, claiming it's a "cheat meal." Spoiler: It's not cheating; it's just carb denial.

Keto isn't inherently bad—it can be effective for weight loss and managing certain medical conditions. But is it sustainable for the average person who enjoys roti and rice? Unlikely. Moderation, not carb elimination, is key.

Paleo: The Caveman Diet

The Paleo diet is all about eating like our ancestors, who supposedly hunted, gathered, and lived carb-free lives of peak health. It bans grains, dairy, legumes, and processed foods while glorifying meats, nuts, and berries. Advocates say it's the secret to weight loss, clear skin, and eternal energy.

But let's be real: the only thing caveman-like about the modern Paleo diet is the occasional urge to bash your plate against the wall out of frustration. While cutting processed foods is commendable, demonizing entire food groups like grains and dairy ignores the fact that humans have evolved to digest these foods. Also, cavemen didn't have almond flour pancakes and grass-fed beef jerky delivered to their caves via app.

Here's the irony: most of the people touting Paleo wouldn't last a week in actual prehistoric conditions. For one, they'd have to chase their meals instead of ordering them online. And good luck maintaining that six-pack when your main protein source is whatever you can catch in your backyard.

Juice Cleanses: Liquid Lies

Juice cleanses promise to detox your body, reset your metabolism, and unleash your inner radiance. All you have to do is spend a small fortune on cold-pressed juices and abstain from solid food for days on end. Sounds appealing, right? Until you realize you've paid the price of a vacation for the privilege of being perpetually hungry and irritable.

Let's debunk this myth once and for all: your liver and kidneys are your detox heroes, working round the clock to eliminate toxins. They don't need a green juice assist. In fact, juice cleanses can do more harm than good, stripping your body of essential proteins, fats, and fiber while flooding it with sugar. That's right—most juices are sugar bombs masquerading as health elixirs. And the weight you lose on a cleanse? Mostly water. It'll return as soon as you reintroduce actual food.

Intermittent Fasting: Skipping Breakfast, but Make It Trendy

Intermittent fasting (IF) is all about timing your meals, with popular methods like the 16:8 plan (16 hours of fasting, 8 hours of eating) or alternate-day fasting. It's hailed as a way to lose weight, improve focus, and regulate blood sugar. But what it often boils down to is skipping breakfast and giving it a fancy name.

IF can work for some people, particularly those who thrive on routine. But for others, it's just a gateway to hanger (hunger-induced anger). Picture this: You're 12 hours into your fast, counting the minutes until your feeding window opens, and someone offers you a plate of fries. Willpower is a myth at that point.

The biggest issue with IF is that it can encourage binge eating during the eating window. If you consume a day's worth of calories in one sitting, you're not exactly doing your body any favours. It's not magic; it's math. If you eat more calories than you burn, fasting won't save you.

Detox Teas and Other Gimmicks

Let's talk about detox teas—those Instagram darlings peddled by influencers promising a flat tummy and glowing skin. What they don't tell you is that these teas often contain laxatives. Sure, you'll lose weight—mostly water and whatever was in your digestive tract—but you'll also gain a dependency on something your body didn't need in the first place.

The detox industry thrives on the false notion that your body is a cesspool of toxins that need purging. Newsflash: Your liver and kidneys have that covered. No tea, powder, or potion can "cleanse" your system better than these hardworking organs. Save your money and invest in something truly cleansing, like a good night's sleep or a solid workout.

Balanced Approaches That Actually Work

The truth is, most diets fail because they're too restrictive, too complicated, or too detached from real life. Sustainable health isn't about eliminating entire food groups or starving yourself. It's about balance, variety, and enjoying food without guilt.

Here are some practical tips:

- **Embrace Moderation**: Love carbs? Have them. Just pair them with protein and fiber to keep your blood sugar stable.

- **Cook at Home**: Preparing your own meals gives you control over ingredients, portion sizes, and cooking methods.

- **Focus on Whole Foods**: Fill your plate with vegetables, fruits, whole grains, and lean proteins. Save indulgences for when they truly feel worth it.

- **Stay Active**: No diet can outpace a sedentary lifestyle. Find a form of movement you enjoy and make it a regular part of your routine.

- **Listen to Your Body**: Hunger isn't the enemy; it's your body's way of asking for fuel. Feed it nourishing foods and stop when you're satisfied.

In the end, the best "diet" is the one you can stick to—not for a week or a month, but for life. It's about making small, consistent changes that add up over time, not jumping on the latest bandwagon. So, the next time someone tries to sell you a magic bullet for weight loss or health, remember: if it sounds too good to be true, it probably is.

Decoding Labels and Claims

Navigating grocery aisles today feels less like shopping and more like decoding hieroglyphics. The brightly coloured boxes and bottles shout buzzwords at you— "organic," "natural," "gluten-free," "superfood." Each claim seems designed to inspire confidence, making you believe you're making the healthiest choice. But here's the uncomfortable truth: most of these labels are marketing traps. They're engineered to tug at your insecurities and desires, capitalizing on the universal wish to eat better, live longer, and maybe, just maybe, squeeze into those pre-pandemic jeans. Yet, when you dig deeper, what you often find is an ingredient list that reads more like a chemistry experiment than a recipe.

The parallels to cookware marketing are uncanny. That non-stick frying pan you bought last year? The one that promised "PFOA-free, eco-friendly, safe at high heat"? It might be harbouring just as many hidden surprises as that low-fat yogurt packed with added sugars. The overlap between misleading food labels and cookware claims is startling. Both industries bank on your good intentions. You want to make healthy meals, so you pick products and tools that seem to promise the best. But how often do we really examine the fine print? Just as the term "natural" on a cereal box doesn't mean free of preservatives or additives, "PFOA-free" doesn't mean the absence of all toxic chemicals in your cookware.

Let's start with food. Labels like "low-fat" or "no added sugar" seem straightforward but often tell only half the story. When manufacturers remove fat from a product, they replace it with sugar or artificial sweeteners to compensate for the lost flavour. That "healthy" low-fat yogurt you tossed into your cart? It could have as much sugar as a candy bar. Similarly, "no added sugar" doesn't mean a product is sugar-free—it could still be loaded with naturally occurring sugars like those in dates, fruit concentrates, or honey. These sugars, while not "added," can still spike your blood sugar levels, especially when consumed in processed forms.

Now think about cookware. Non-stick pans have been a staple in kitchens for years, promising quick clean-ups and perfect omelettes. But behind that convenience lies a world of hidden risks. When overheated, many non-stick surfaces can release toxic fumes, potentially harmful to both humans and pets. The phrase "PFOA-free," which you might have spotted on your latest pan purchase, only guarantees the absence of one specific chemical. It doesn't account for the many other unregulated substances manufacturers may use instead. Much like sneaky sugars in your food, harmful chemicals in cookware are often swapped for less notorious—but still questionable—alternatives.

To make informed choices, you must dig deeper than the bold claims plastered on the front of products. Flip that box over. Look at the ingredients list and the nutrition facts. On a jar of "all-natural" peanut butter, you might expect just peanuts and maybe salt, but don't be surprised to find hydrogenated oils or added sugars. Similarly, examine the care instructions and materials of your cookware. Does that "ceramic-coated" pan truly avoid toxins, or does it begin to degrade after just a few months of use, exposing a questionable base material?

The language of food and cookware marketing thrives on vagueness. Take "natural," one of the most abused terms in the industry. You'd think it implies a product free of artificial chemicals, but in reality, it's a loosely regulated term. A "natural" granola bar can still contain high-fructose corn syrup, as long as the sweetener originally came from corn. Likewise, a "safe" non-stick pan might mean it's safe under specific conditions—like not exceeding 500°F, which is laughable for anyone who sears, sautés, or forgets the stove is on while chatting on the phone.

And then there's the allure of buzzwords like "superfood" or "gluten-free." While these terms suggest superior nutrition or health benefits, they're often more about marketing than substance. "Superfood" isn't a regulated term—it's just a way to make kale sound sexier than spinach or to justify the steep price of goji berries. Similarly, "gluten-free" doesn't necessarily mean healthy. A gluten-free cookie might be free of wheat, but it can still be packed with refined carbs, sugar, and unhealthy fats. It's the same with cookware marketed as "eco-friendly" or "sustainable." A label might tout green credentials, but if the pan's coating flakes off into your food within months, how sustainable was that choice?

Let's not forget portion control, another deceptive tactic both food and cookware industries exploit. Manufacturers often manipulate serving sizes to make their products appear healthier. That innocent-looking bag of chips boasting "only 150 calories" per serving? Check the fine print, and you'll realize the bag contains three servings—an easy trap if you're snacking mindlessly. Similarly, cookware advertisements often fail to address longevity. A pan marketed as "lifetime safe" may last a year before showing wear that compromises its supposed non-toxicity. Just as with food, the devil is in the details, and understanding those details is crucial.

If the food label rabbit hole seems overwhelming, take a moment to think about your kitchen as a whole. We often focus so much on what goes onto our plates that we overlook what happens before it gets there. A meticulously chosen organic vegetable sautéed in a pan releasing harmful fumes feels like the culinary equivalent of cancelling out your morning run with a double cheeseburger. The solution isn't paranoia—it's curiosity. Much like learning to identify hidden sugars or decipher ambiguous health claims, understanding your cookware can empower you to make better choices.

Start small. Swap non-stick pans for cast iron or stainless steel, both of which are free of chemical coatings and can last for decades if cared for properly. Look for labels like "100% ceramic" rather than "ceramic coated." If you're investing in cookware, ensure it aligns with your health goals, just as you would with food. After all, what good is carefully avoiding refined oils or added sugars if your pan is contributing microscopic particles to your meal?

The real takeaway here isn't to distrust every product you see but to approach both food and cookware labels with a critical eye. Ask questions. Why is this pan labelled "eco-friendly"? What's behind the "natural Flavors" listed on this snack? Do I really need that imported quinoa, or can I get similar nutrition from locally grown millets? By challenging assumptions and reading beyond the buzzwords, you reclaim control over your kitchen and, ultimately, your health.

Your kitchen is a sanctuary—one where love, health, and creativity converge. The choices you make about what to cook and how to cook it have ripple effects on your well-being. Marketing may try to blur those lines with flashy claims and strategic packaging, but with a bit of awareness, you can cut through the noise. So, the next time you're in the grocery aisle or browsing cookware online, remember: it's not just about what looks good on the surface. Healthy eating and cooking start with what's real, what's durable, and what truly nourishes—not just in the short term but for years to come.

PART III

Building a Sustainable, Joyful Relationship with Food

Chapter 6

Building a Healthier Relationship with Food

The Joy and Cultural Significance of Food

Food is more than sustenance; it's the thread that weaves through our lives, connecting us to our culture, family, and memories. From childhood snacks to elaborate holiday feasts, food is entwined with the most cherished moments of our existence. It's a silent witness to our joys and sorrows, a comforting companion in times of uncertainty, and a canvas for creativity and celebration. In every bite, there's a story—a recipe passed down generations, a technique perfected over time, or a flavour that speaks to a specific region or tradition.

Take a moment to think about the dishes that have shaped your memories. Maybe it's the warmth of parathas on a lazy Sunday morning, served with dollops of butter by a doting grandmother. Perhaps it's the unmistakable aroma of a family recipe during festive celebrations, or the simplicity of rice and dal after a long day. These meals do more than fill us up; they ground us. They remind us of where we come from and who we are.

In cultures around the world, food is the centrepiece of connection. In Italy, the art of making fresh pasta brings families together, with each step passed down as an unspoken legacy. In India, the act of rolling rotis is a shared ritual, often accompanied by conversations and laughter. Across continents, food transcends its utilitarian role, becoming a universal language of love and care.

Yet, in modern times, our relationship with food has become strained. In the rush of daily life, food often gets reduced to calories, macros, and meal prep schedules. Meals are no longer shared experiences but hurried breaks between tasks, often consumed in front of screens or on the go. The joy of eating has been overshadowed by guilt, driven by diet culture's relentless messages to count, measure, and restrict. In this fragmented approach, food risks losing its soul.

But what if we reclaimed it? Imagine approaching food not as a chore but as a celebration. Every meal is an opportunity to pause and appreciate the effort, history, and artistry that brought it to your plate. A single sip of tea can transport you to quiet mornings, while the crunch of fresh vegetables connects you to the earth's abundance. Eating becomes more than a biological necessity; it's an act of gratitude and mindfulness.

Cultural traditions around food are a powerful way to reconnect with its joy. Think about the symbolic significance of meals in festivals—the sweet indulgence of modaks during Ganesh Chaturthi, the rich biryanis of Eid feasts, or the tangy pickles that bring a burst of nostalgia with every bite. These dishes carry the wisdom of generations, crafted with care and infused with meaning. They're not just recipes; they're rituals, tying us to our roots and helping us navigate the modern world with a sense of belonging.

The communal nature of food is another source of its magic. Cooking together strengthens bonds, turning mundane tasks into moments of connection. Sharing meals fosters understanding, whether around a dining table or during a potluck. Even the act of exchanging recipes is an act of trust, an invitation to experience someone else's culture or history.

As we navigate the complexities of modern life, food remains a constant—a reminder of simpler times, of connections that transcend words. It's an antidote to loneliness and an anchor in a world that often feels unsteady. It reminds us that even amidst chaos, there's beauty in the act of nourishing ourselves and others.

Reclaiming the joy and cultural significance of food starts with intention. Make time to savour meals, even on the busiest days. Honour the dishes that shaped your identity, and explore those that can broaden your horizons. Share your table, whether with loved ones or strangers, because food has a way of breaking down barriers and building bridges. It's a universal truth: when we come together over a meal, we're reminded of our shared humanity.

Let food be more than just what's on your plate. Let it be the stories it tells, the memories it holds, and the connections it fosters. In its simplest and grandest forms, food is a celebration—a testament to resilience, creativity, and love. And it's always worth savouring.

Mindful Eating: The Art of Savouring Every Bite

Mindful eating is a quiet revolution in how we approach food, challenging the fast-paced habits of modern life. It invites us to turn meals into moments of connection, not just with the food on our plates but also with ourselves. In a world obsessed with calories, macros, and the next trendy diet, mindful eating is a refreshing reminder that food isn't just fuel—it's an experience.

Picture the joy of biting into a fresh slice of bread, the vibrant hues of a summer salad, or the comforting aroma of hot tea. These are simple pleasures often overshadowed by our distracted eating habits. It's time to reclaim them.

Mindful eating begins with awareness and intention. It's not about rules or restrictions; it's about being present. It starts with asking questions: Why am I eating? Am I hungry, bored, or stressed?

How does this food make me feel? The answers often reveal more than we expect. This practice is also about letting go of judgment. Food isn't "good" or "bad," and neither are our choices. If you indulge in a decadent dessert, savour it. There's no room for guilt at the mindful table—just curiosity and balance.

But how often do we truly notice our food? In today's world, meals are multitasking opportunities—paired with emails, binge-watching, or scrolling social media. These distractions rob us of the simple joy of eating. They also disconnect us from our body's natural hunger and fullness cues, leaving us unsatisfied and prone to overeating. When was the last time you truly tasted your food without rushing through it? Even something as ordinary as a buttered slice of toast can feel indulgent if you slow down and savour it.

To practice mindful eating, begin by pausing before a meal. Take a deep breath. Look at the food in front of you—its colours, textures, and arrangement. Take in its aroma. Then, with your first bite, immerse yourself in the flavours and sensations. Chew slowly, allowing the taste to linger. This simple act transforms eating from a mechanical task into a sensory experience. Putting down your fork between bites and eating without distractions can further enhance this practice, making every meal a mindful moment.

This approach has profound benefits, both physical and emotional. Slowing down and chewing thoroughly aids digestion, reducing common discomforts like bloating. It also gives your brain time to register fullness, helping you naturally avoid overeating. Mindful eating can even transform your relationship with food. When you stop categorising meals as indulgences or cheats, you learn to appreciate them for what they truly are—sources of nourishment and joy. Over time, this shift reduces emotional eating, as you become better at distinguishing physical hunger from cravings driven by stress or boredom.

Food tastes better when we pay attention. The spices in a curry, the sweetness of a ripe mango, or the tang of fresh yoghurt all become more pronounced. When we eat mindfully, smaller portions satisfy because we fully experience their richness. This helps us embrace balance naturally, without the need for strict diets or complicated plans.

Of course, we live in a busy world, and practising mindful eating doesn't mean every meal must be a drawn-out ceremony. It's about finding mindful moments where they fit. Start small—choose one meal or snack a day to eat without distractions. Even a morning cup of tea can become a mindful ritual if you savour each sip and take in its warmth and aroma.

Mindful eating isn't about getting it right all the time. Life is messy, and there will be rushed meals and distracted snacking. What matters is the overall mindset—a willingness to slow down when possible and approach food with gratitude and presence. This practice enriches not just our eating habits but also our appreciation for life's simpler pleasures.

By cultivating mindfulness at mealtimes, we turn ordinary moments into extraordinary ones. The act of eating becomes a celebration—of the food, the people who prepared it, and the body it nourishes. In this way, mindful eating offers more than satisfaction; it offers a way of being, a slower, more intentional rhythm that brings joy and connection to every bite. It's a reminder that food is not just a necessity but a profound pleasure, waiting to be rediscovered in every meal.

Creating Joyful Eating Rituals

Mealtime can be more than just a moment to satisfy hunger; it can be transformed into a ritual that nourishes not just the body but also the mind and soul. Imagine turning every meal into an experience, a small celebration of flavour, tradition, and connection. With a little intention, even the most routine meals can become a source of joy and mindfulness.

The first step is to set the scene. Think of the difference between hurriedly eating a sandwich over the sink and sitting down at a neatly arranged table with a proper plate, utensils, and maybe a vase of flowers. The food might be the same, but the experience transforms. A well-set table doesn't need to be fancy—it could be as simple as unfolding a napkin, lighting a candle, or using your favourite plate. These small gestures elevate the meal, reminding you that it's worth taking a moment to appreciate what you're about to eat.

Ambience plays a crucial role in creating these rituals. Consider the effect of soft music in the background or eating by natural light at a sunny window. Even the simplest meal becomes a sensory experience when you engage all five senses. The sight of vibrant colours on your plate, the aroma of freshly cooked food, the sound of a gentle breeze or light chatter, the texture of crispy bread or tender vegetables, and of course, the taste of the meal itself—each element contributes to a richer, more satisfying eating experience.

Food isn't just about sustenance; it's deeply tied to memory and tradition. Every family has its stories, often told through recipes passed down from one generation to the next. Perhaps it's a grandmother's secret spice blend for curry, or the way your father taught you to knead dough just right for rotis. These traditions connect us to our roots, grounding us in the legacy of those who came before us.

Incorporating these personal or cultural traditions into your daily meals can be a beautiful way to add meaning. Maybe it's making your mother's signature soup on Sundays or trying your hand at a dish you loved as a child. By revisiting these recipes, you keep those memories alive, infusing your meals with nostalgia and gratitude.

A great way to bring consistency and joy to mealtime is to establish a weekly rhythm. Consider designating specific days for certain culinary themes. Perhaps Friday becomes "comfort food night," where you prepare a dish that feels indulgent and cosy, like homemade mac and cheese or your favourite biryani. Wednesdays could be "leftover transformation day," where you reinvent extra ingredients into new, exciting dishes. Imagine turning yesterday's roasted vegetables into a vibrant pasta or transforming dal into a hearty soup.

Theme days add structure to your week while sparking creativity. They reduce decision fatigue (you know what's coming up) and make even ordinary weeks feel special. For families, involving everyone in planning or preparing meals can turn these nights into bonding moments. Children can help choose themes or decorate the table, adding their touch to the ritual.

Of course, treats deserve their place in the rhythm. Indulgences should never be a source of guilt; they're a vital part of balanced eating. Whether it's a decadent dessert, a buttery croissant, or a packet of crisps, treats are more enjoyable when they're anticipated and savoured. Planning these indulgences lets you fully embrace them without the shadow of regret.

Quality often matters more than quantity when it comes to treats. A small piece of dark chocolate, rich and satisfying, can be far more fulfilling than a large, overly sweet bar. Savouring each bite, letting the flavours linger, makes the experience more rewarding. Treats are about joy, not excess, and when they're part of your weekly plan, they feel like a celebration rather than a slip.

These joyful eating rituals can also act as anchors, grounding us during chaotic times. When life feels overwhelming, a familiar meal routine or a beautifully set table can provide comfort and stability. Food becomes a source of calm, reminding us to slow down, appreciate the present moment, and connect with ourselves and our loved ones.

As you start creating these rituals, remember that they don't have to be perfect or elaborate. A small gesture, like pausing to take a breath before eating or lighting a candle at dinner, can be enough to bring mindfulness and joy to the experience. Over time, these moments become habits, enriching your relationship with food and making each meal something to look forward to.

The beauty of these rituals lies in their flexibility. Whether you live alone, with a partner, or in a bustling household, they can be adapted to suit your life. You might not always have the time to set a full table or prepare a traditional dish, and that's okay. The goal is to approach meals with intention, creating a little space in your day to honour the food you eat and the time you spend enjoying it.

Through these small but meaningful practices, eating becomes more than a daily necessity. It transforms into an art—an opportunity to celebrate, connect, and take pleasure in life's simplest yet most essential act.

Chapter 7

The Spice Route – Reclaiming the Indian Masala Shelf

The Healing Power of Indian Spices – Not Your Average Medicine Cabinet

Indian spices aren't just ingredients; they're cultural icons. For centuries, they've been the superheroes of our kitchens, blending culinary delight with medicinal might. These spices are multitaskers, healing everything from runny noses to broken hearts. And yes, they've been long-standing remedies for bruised egos too—try giving someone haldi doodh after they've had a bad day. Each spice has its own personality, quirks, and an extensive résumé of health benefits that's been celebrated across the subcontinent. Let's dive into this colourful, aromatic world where every pinch carries a legacy.

Take turmeric, for example. Turmeric isn't just a spice; it's the golden diva of the masala shelf. It shows up in everything from your grandma's wound-healing concoctions to fancy turmeric lattes priced like gold dust in trendy cafés. Growing up, no Indian child escaped the universal truth: a scraped knee meant two things— stinging antiseptic and a turmeric paste that turned the wound (and your skin) bright yellow. Beyond the kitchen, turmeric has also been revered in rituals, ceremonies, and Ayurvedic practices. Whether it's South India's rasam or Punjab's ghee-laden sabzis, this spice has been flaunting its glow for centuries. What the West calls a superfood, we've always known as haldi, our humble go-to healer.

Then there's cumin, the understated yet indispensable spice in every Indian household. Cumin doesn't seek attention, but it's the quiet overachiever that holds the dish together. Its earthy aroma makes Andhra biryanis sing and Gujarat's chaas soothing on a summer afternoon. Jeera isn't just about taste; it's a digestive champion. That tiny seed has the power to turn a post-meal stomach grumble into a peaceful sigh. A quick tadka of cumin in hot ghee is like a culinary hug—subtle yet comforting.

Meanwhile, cardamom, the elegant queen of the spice world, brings sophistication to every dish. Whether it's elevating Kerala's creamy payasams or Kolkata's mishti doi, elaichi knows how to make an entrance. Growing up, cardamom pods were often treated like treasure, tucked away in spice jars and rationed with care. A whiff of cardamom can turn chai into a celebration and transform a simple dessert into a royal treat. It's the kind of spice that walks into a room and steals the show, leaving everyone wondering how they lived without it.

And then we have cinnamon, the sweet-talking rogue that spices up your life. Cinnamon's versatility is astonishing—it brings warmth to Kashmiri rogan josh and adds zing to chai that warms your soul on a cold winter evening. But cinnamon isn't just about flavour; it's a health star. Packed with antioxidants and known for stabilising blood sugar, it's become a darling of both traditional kitchens and Instagram feeds. While the West waxes poetic about its health benefits, Indian homes have been dropping cinnamon sticks into curries for centuries, no fanfare needed.

If spices were a family, black pepper would be the older sibling who's been around the block. Often overshadowed by newer, trendier flavours, black pepper is the OG superfood. Dubbed "black gold" in Kerala, it once fuelled trade routes and shaped empires. But in the kitchen, pepper has a simpler role: adding heat and depth to dishes. From Bengal's machher jhol to Tamil Nadu's milagu rasam, this unassuming spice punches above its weight. It's the go-to cure for everything from colds to bland food. A sprinkle of pepper is like a wake-up call for your taste buds—and sometimes, your sinuses.

Cloves and coriander are the unsung workhorses of the masala family, always ready to step up and deliver. Cloves bring their intense, slightly sweet flavour to chai, pulaos, and garam masala, while also moonlighting as a remedy for toothaches. Coriander, whether as seeds or fresh leaves, is the cheerful multitasker. It brightens everything it touches, from Konkani fish curries to Delhi's iconic chaat. Together, these spices quietly uphold the culinary traditions of a nation without asking for the limelight.

What makes Indian spices even more fascinating is how they mirror the diversity of the country itself. Each region brings its own twist to spice usage, creating a mosaic of flavours. From Karnataka's fiery Byadgi chillies to Rajasthan's amchoor (dried mango powder), every spice tells a story of geography, climate, and culture. These regional heroes bring depth and vibrancy to Indian cooking, reminding us that food is as much about identity as it is about sustenance.

Take saffron, for instance, the jewel of Kashmiri cuisine. Known for its rich colour and delicate aroma, saffron is a spice of luxury and tradition. Its threads are often steeped in milk to create luscious dishes like kheer or added to biryanis for a fragrant touch. Then there's the humble mustard seed, a staple in Bengali and South Indian kitchens. Its sharp, pungent flavour is essential in tempering dals, pickles, and even fish curries, showcasing its versatility and importance.

Indian spices aren't just pantry staples; they're carriers of tradition, health, and history. They've been around long before wellness trends and will remain long after the next superfood hype fades. The magic lies not only in their flavours but in their ability to connect generations and regions, all while adding warmth and vitality to our lives. So, the next time you reach for that jar of turmeric or cumin, remember—you're not just cooking. You're participating in a legacy as rich and enduring as the spices themselves.

Masala Magic: Quick Tips to Spice Up Your Life

Spices can seem as intimidating as an ancient recipe book written in a language you don't quite understand. But fear not—masalas are not out to overwhelm you. They're the life of the kitchen party, ready to jazz up your meals and make you look like a seasoned chef even when your cooking skills are, let's say, "experimental." The truth is, spices are forgiving, endlessly fun, and surprisingly easy to work with once you dive in.

Think of masalas as mood enhancers for food. Feeling lazy? Toss in a dash of garam masala, and your rice suddenly feels like it belongs on a restaurant menu. Bored of bland veggies? A sprinkle of chaat masala, and voila—you've got yourself a tangy masterpiece. Whether you're a confident cook or someone who thinks salt and pepper are adventurous, masalas are here to make your kitchen life easier, tastier, and infinitely more fun.

Take garam masala, for example. This iconic North Indian blend is like the all-rounder friend who's good at everything. It's warm, aromatic, and packed with spices like cinnamon, cloves, and cardamom. But don't let its fancy reputation fool you—garam masala is as easy to use as pressing "shuffle" on a playlist. Add it at the end of cooking to curries, soups, or even roasted chickpeas, and watch your dish transform from average to exceptional.

If garam masala is the headliner, chaat masala is the cheeky sidekick. Tangy, salty, and just a little funky (thanks to black salt), it's the spice equivalent of that friend who knows how to liven up any situation. Got a sad fruit salad? Sprinkle some chaat masala.

Leftover fries? Sprinkle some more. It's even been known to rescue lacklustre instant noodles. Honestly, it's like magic dust in a bottle.

Now let's talk about sambhar podi—the South Indian spice mix that proves breakfast is serious business. Sambhar, with its warm, tangy, and slightly spicy flavours, owes its charm to this complex blend of lentils, coriander, and dried chillies. But sambhar podi isn't just for sambhar. Sprinkle it on roasted veggies, add it to dosa batter, or even mix it with plain yoghurt for a quick dip. It's versatile, bold, and guaranteed to make you rethink your spice limits.

For those who like things simple but effective, panch phoron is the way to go. This Bengali five-spice mix—fennel, cumin, mustard, fenugreek, and nigella seeds—is a minimalist's dream. Toss it into hot oil to release its nutty, earthy aroma, then add to dals, stir-fries, or even soups for an instant flavour boost. It's proof that sometimes, less really is more.

And let's not overlook turmeric, the golden spice that's been stealing global headlines thanks to its "superfood" status. Sure, the world may call it a turmeric latte, but we know it as good old haldi doodh—the bedtime drink your grandma swore by. But turmeric isn't just trendy; it's a true kitchen hero. It's warm, earthy flavour and vibrant yellow hue make it the star of curries, pulaos, and even homemade pickles. Plus, it pairs beautifully with black pepper, which boosts its health benefits. A pinch of turmeric, a dash of pepper, and suddenly, you're cooking like a pro.

Speaking of black pepper, let's give this spice its due. Known as "black gold" in Kerala, pepper is the quiet achiever of the masala world. It's spicy without being overpowering, and it complements everything from creamy soups to crispy fish. Grind it fresh, and you'll wonder how you ever lived without it. Fun fact: black pepper was once so valuable it was used as currency. So, the next time you add a pinch to your curry, take a moment to feel just a little fancy.

Of course, no discussion of Indian masalas is complete without a nod to the workhorses: cumin and coriander. These spices are like the backbone of Indian cooking, quietly supporting everything from Punjabi chole to Gujarati kadhi. Cumin, with its warm, earthy notes, is a digestive powerhouse and a flavour booster. Coriander, meanwhile, brings a bright, citrusy touch to spice blends, marinades, and even chutneys. Together, they're the dependable duo you didn't know you needed.

If all this sounds overwhelming, don't worry—Indian spices are more about intuition than instruction. You don't need a full spice rack or a PhD in culinary arts to use them. Start small. Pick one or two blends, like garam masala or sambhar podi, and experiment. Add a little, taste, and adjust. Indian cooking is forgiving, flexible, and fun—just like its spices.

For the truly spice-shy, here's a pro tip: when in doubt, "garam masala it out." Seriously, this blend is so versatile it's like the little black dress of Indian cooking. Or, if you're feeling bold, try chaat masala—it's practically a party in a bottle. These blends are your entry points into the world of masalas, ready to rescue any meal that's teetering on the edge of mediocrity.

But let's also acknowledge that cooking with spices is as much about confidence as it is about technique. Don't stress about getting it "right." Spices are there to enhance, not intimidate. And if you mess up? Just sprinkle some more chaat masala on top and call it a day. After all, cooking is meant to be joyful, messy, and delicious.

Masalas aren't just ingredients—they're little bursts of culture, history, and flavour packed into tiny jars. They remind us that food isn't just about sustenance; it's about stories, memories, and a whole lot of spice-induced laughter. So, grab your masala tin, roll up your sleeves, and let the magic begin. Because with the right spices, every meal can be a masterpiece.

Spicing Up Your Life (Without Poisoning It)

Spices are magical—they bring warmth, depth, and nostalgia to every dish they touch. But as with all great things, there's always a catch. Recently, headlines about adulterated spices have been enough to make us rethink that cheerful sprinkle of garam masala. From pesticide-laden turmeric to cloves spiked with questionable additives, the spice world has had its fair share of scandals. But does that mean we give up on our beloved masalas? Absolutely not. It just means we need to spice smarter, not scarier.

Imagine this: you're cooking a lovely curry, humming along, and suddenly you see a news report that some brands of coriander powder contain fillers. Fillers! Who knew spices could have trust issues? And then there's the turmeric that's been bulked up with harmful dyes. It's enough to make you clutch your masala tin protectively. But don't worry. There's a way to keep the magic of spices alive in your kitchen without playing detective every time you shop.

Let's start with the golden rule: quality over convenience. Whole spices, like cumin seeds or black peppercorns, are your safest bet. They're less likely to be adulterated, and they pack a punch of freshness that pre-ground versions often lose. Plus, there's something oddly satisfying about grinding your own spices—it's like a mini workout with a fragrant reward. If you're feeling adventurous, invest in a small spice grinder and unleash your inner culinary scientist. Imagine the bragging rights when you casually mention at dinner, "Oh, I ground the garam masala myself."

But let's be real grinding your own spices isn't always practical, especially when life feels like a never-ending episode of "Chopped." In those moments, trusted brands are your best friends. Look for labels that boast certifications, like FSSAI in India or organic stamps globally. It's not just about safety; it's about supporting companies that respect the integrity of spices. Sure, they might cost a little more, but think of it as an investment in both your health and the legacy of Indian cooking.

Still, even with trustworthy brands, it's smart to stay vigilant. Here's a quick trick: the sniff test. Fresh spices have a distinctive aroma that hits you immediately. If your ground turmeric smells faint or your cumin seems shy, it's probably been sitting around longer than it should. And don't forget to check for clumps—moisture is the enemy of spices, turning them into sad, damp powders. Store them in airtight containers, away from light and heat, to keep their flavour and potency intact.

Now, let's address the elephant in the room: the cost of "pure" spices. Yes, Kashmiri saffron is expensive enough to make you reconsider your life choices, and organic turmeric could rival your grocery bill for an entire week. But here's the thing—spices are used sparingly, so a little goes a long way. Instead of skimping on quality, buy smaller quantities of the good stuff. It's like buying fancy chocolate: you don't need a lot to feel indulgent.

Speaking of indulgence, let's not forget the regional spice heroes that deserve their moment in the spotlight. From Kerala's pepper to Karnataka's Byadgi chillies, these local treasures have been elevating Indian cooking for centuries. By supporting these regional varieties, you're not just cooking with authenticity—you're also helping preserve the agricultural traditions of India. Plus, you get to feel smug about using something a Michelin-star chef might describe as "locally sourced."

Of course, no discussion of spices is complete without poking a little fun at how the West has suddenly discovered their "superfood" status. Turmeric latte? We've been drinking haldi doodh since forever. Cumin detox water? Hello, we call that jeera paani, and it's been the go-to remedy for upset stomachs since before anyone knew what "detox" even meant. But hey, if global hype means more love for Indian spices, who are we to complain? Just don't let anyone tell you that $7 turmeric tea is revolutionary—it's basically your nani's bedtime routine with a fancy price tag.

While we're on the topic of trends, let's address the art of balancing spices in your cooking. Too much garam masala can turn a dish bitter, while overloading on turmeric can make everything taste like medicine. The key is to start small. Think of spices like personality traits—you want a little sass, not an overwhelming smack of drama. Taste as you go, and remember that you can always add more, but taking it out? That's a kitchen heartbreak waiting to happen.

And for those who've ever panicked in front of a spice rack, here's a tip: you don't need to use all the spices all the time. Some of the best dishes are simple. A pinch of cumin, a hint of turmeric, and a sprinkle of salt can work wonders. Indian cooking isn't about complexity; it's about balance. Even a basic tadka can turn plain dal into a bowl of comfort.

Now, let's tackle the ultimate question: whole spices or ground? It's a bit like dating—whole spices are raw and authentic, while pre-ground ones are convenient but can lose their spark over time. The answer? A mix of both. Use whole spices when you want to impress (or when you have time) and keep a few reliable ground blends for busy days. After all, balance is the spice of life.

So, what have we learned? Spices are amazing, but they're not perfect. They need a little care, a touch of caution, and a whole lot of appreciation. By choosing wisely, storing them well, and embracing their quirks, you can enjoy everything they bring to the table—without the stress of wondering if your masala is more filler than flavour.

Indian spices aren't just ingredients; they're a celebration of tradition, creativity, and sheer deliciousness. So, the next time you reach for that pinch of cinnamon or dash of black pepper, do it with confidence. Because with a little awareness and a lot of love, spices will continue to work their magic—one dish at a time.

Chapter 8

Cooking the Indian Way – Rediscovering Ancestral Techniques

Rediscovering the Art of Slow Cooking

In a world where efficiency reigns supreme, where meals are hurried and instant gratification is the norm, slow cooking stands as a quiet rebellion. It is an ode to patience, a love letter to the flavours that can only be coaxed out with time. In the realm of Indian cooking, slow cooking isn't just a method; it's a tradition steeped in culture, wisdom, and sensory indulgence. Long before fast food chains and pre-packaged dinners took over our schedules, the Indian kitchen was a sanctuary where time was a critical ingredient. The slow simmering of a dal or the gentle cooking of a curry wasn't just about food; it was about creating an experience that nourished the soul as much as the body.

Imagine the rich aroma of a dal makhani, slowly bubbling on a stove for hours, its creamy texture and layered flavours coming to life with each passing moment. Think of a biryani, with its carefully arranged layers of rice and meat, sealed tightly and cooked on dum, allowing the steam to weave magic. These are dishes that don't just fill a plate; they tell stories of heritage, skill, and love. Slow cooking allows ingredients to reach their fullest potential, each spice releasing its essence, every vegetable or piece of meat breaking down into tender perfection.

The beauty of slow cooking lies in its ability to elevate the simplest ingredients. A few lentils, a handful of spices, and some patience can create a dish that rivals the most elaborate feasts. Take the humble khichdi, for instance. A dish of rice and lentils, slow cooked with mild spices and a dollop of ghee, transforms into a bowl of comfort that soothes the body and mind. Or the traditional dal makhani, where lentils and kidney beans simmer for hours until they achieve a luscious, creamy consistency that is pure indulgence. It's not just about the time spent but the intention behind it, the love poured into every stirring of the pot.

In Indian kitchens, slow cooking is often a communal affair, an opportunity to connect with family and tradition. It's about sitting around the kitchen, sharing stories while a pot of curry bubbles away, the air rich with the heady mix of spices. It's about layering a biryani while recounting memories of festivals past or grinding masalas by hand while chatting about the day's events. Slow cooking transforms meals from mere sustenance into rituals, where the process is as fulfilling as the result.

But why does slow cooking hold such a special place in Indian cuisine? It's not just about taste, although the flavours are undeniably unparalleled. It's also about the science behind it. When spices are exposed to gentle heat over time, they release essential oils that deepen the flavour profile of a dish. Lentils and legumes, when simmered slowly, develop a creamy texture without the need for artificial thickeners. Meats become tender and infused with the spices around them, each bite a burst of complexity and warmth. Even vegetables, when cooked slowly, retain their natural sweetness and absorb the rich flavours of the curry they're nestled in.

Consider the mutton in a rogan josh, a Kashmiri delicacy where the meat is marinated in yogurt and spices before being simmered for hours. The result is a dish where the meat practically melts in your mouth, every bite a harmony of heat and depth. Or the creamy dal makhani, a signature dish of Punjab, where whole black lentils and kidney beans are cooked overnight, enriched with butter and cream. It's the kind of food that comforts and satisfies, not just because of its taste but because of the time and care that went into its creation.

The joy of slow cooking isn't just limited to elaborate meals. Even simple dishes benefit from this unhurried approach. A basic potato curry, when allowed to cook gently, develops a richness and depth that quick frying could never achieve. A pot of sambhar, simmered slowly with tamarind, vegetables, and freshly ground spices, takes on a complexity that makes every spoonful a delight. Slow cooking invites you to savour not just the meal but the process of creating it, to find beauty in the act of waiting.

In today's fast-paced world, where convenience often takes precedence, slow cooking can feel like a luxury. But it doesn't have to mean spending hours in the kitchen. It's about finding small ways to incorporate the principles of slow cooking into your routine. A weekend dal simmering on the stove while you catch up on chores or a biryani cooked on dum while you read a book can bring the magic of slow cooking into even the busiest lives. Pressure cookers and slow cookers offer modern solutions that capture the essence of traditional methods without the time commitment. Cook under pressure, then let the dish rest on low heat to infuse the flavours fully.

There's also something profoundly meditative about slow cooking. It encourages mindfulness, a connection to the food you're creating. The act of stirring a pot, watching spices bloom in oil, or simply waiting for a dish to reach its peak can be grounding, a reminder to pause and appreciate the present moment. It's a way to reclaim time in a world that constantly demands us to hurry.

Slow cooking is an act of love—for the food, for the people you're cooking for, and for yourself. It's a way of honouring the ingredients, coaxing out their best, and creating something that's more than just a meal. It's a celebration of tradition and a nod to a simpler time when food was more than just fuel; it was an experience, a memory, a joy.

So, the next time you're in the kitchen, consider slowing down. Let the dal simmer a little longer, the spices bloom a little deeper, the curry thicken a little more. Rediscover the magic of slow cooking, not just for the flavours it creates but for the connection it fosters— to your food, your roots, and yourself. It's not just about cooking; it's about savouring every moment, every aroma, every bite. Slow cooking is a journey, one that's worth every second

Reclaiming Forgotten Tools: Mortar, Pestle, and Clay Pots

In an age dominated by high-speed blenders, non-stick pans, and electric grinders, the quiet charm of traditional kitchen tools often goes unnoticed. Yet, nestled in cupboards and storerooms across India, tools like the mortar and pestle, sil-batta, and clay pots stand as timeless relics of culinary artistry. These tools, once the backbone of Indian kitchens, are not mere utensils; they are vessels of culture, heritage, and flavours that machines simply cannot replicate.

Using these tools isn't just about nostalgia—it's about reconnecting with a slower, more mindful approach to cooking. Each tool brings its unique touch, enhancing the texture, aroma, and taste of the dishes they help create. They demand more effort but reward it with a depth of flavour and authenticity that modern gadgets often fall short of delivering. Let's dive into these forgotten heroes and rediscover why they deserve a place in every kitchen.

The Mortar and Pestle: A Symphony of Aromas

The mortar and pestle, known as *hamam dasta* or *khal batta* in many parts of India, is the quintessential spice-grinding tool. It's as much about creating flavours as it is about creating memories—watching your grandmother crush garlic and ginger into a paste or grind cumin and coriander seeds for the day's curry.

Unlike electric grinders, the mortar and pestle don't pulverise ingredients indiscriminately. They crush gently, releasing essential oils and preserving the integrity of the flavours. When you grind fresh black pepper, cardamom, or cloves by hand, the difference is palpable. The aroma is sharper, the flavour more pronounced, and the experience more satisfying.

Regional cuisines across India owe much of their distinctiveness to the mortar and pestle. In Gujarat, for instance, green chutneys are often ground fresh, their zingy flavours preserved by this slow process. Down south, coconut-based masalas for dishes like *kootu* or *avial* benefit immensely from the coarse, textured paste this tool creates. Using a mortar and pestle isn't just a method; it's a ritual, one that invites you to slow down and savour the act of cooking.

Sil-Batta: The Stone-Cold Legend

The *sil-batta*, a flat stone slab with a rolling pin-like stone, is a cousin to the mortar and pestle but takes grinding to another level. In many households, it was the go-to tool for making masalas, chutneys, and wet pastes. The rhythmic grinding motion on the stone doesn't just crush; it coaxes out flavours that no machine can replicate.

A freshly ground coconut chutney on a sil-batta has a texture and taste that blenders simply can't achieve. The friction and heat generated by hand ensure the oils from spices are released evenly, creating layers of complexity in the final dish. In Kerala, *thenga chammanthi* (coconut chutney) or *ulli chammanthi* (onion chutney) are traditionally ground this way, making them earthy and flavourful.

Clay Pots: Earth's Gift to Cooking

Clay pots, or *matkas* and *handis*, are perhaps the most poetic tools of all. They are not just containers but collaborators in the cooking process, imparting a unique earthy flavour to dishes. Their porous nature allows steam to circulate, which tenderises food evenly and keeps it moist. Slow cooking in a clay pot isn't just about the technique; it's about the result—a deep, satisfying flavour that feels as nourishing as it tastes.

In Bengal, clay pots are traditionally used to prepare *mishti doi*, the beloved sweet yoghurt. The porous walls of the pot absorb excess moisture, thickening the yoghurt naturally. Similarly, in the southern states, curries like *meen kuzhambu* (fish curry) are often cooked in clay pots to give the dish its signature smoky, rustic flavour.

Clay pots aren't just for savoury dishes. Across India, they are used for sweet treats like *payasam* and *khichdi*, where the gentle heat distribution prevents scorching and allows the flavours to meld beautifully. And if you've ever sipped water stored in a *matka* on a hot summer day, you'll know there's no better way to quench your thirst.

Why These Tools Matter Today

Beyond nostalgia, there are practical reasons to reclaim these tools. They are more sustainable than their electric counterparts, don't rely on electricity, and often last decades. They also encourage mindful cooking. When you're grinding spices by hand or slow cooking in a clay pot, you're involved in every step of the process, connecting deeply with your ingredients.

Using these tools can also improve the nutritional value of your meals. The slow grinding of spices prevents the loss of essential oils, while clay pots' alkaline nature neutralises acidity in food, enhancing its overall health benefits. It's a win-win for flavour and well-being.

Bringing Traditional Tools to Modern Kitchens

Reintroducing these tools into a busy lifestyle doesn't mean abandoning convenience altogether. Start small. Use a mortar and pestle for fresh spices or a quick garlic-ginger paste. Invest in a small clay pot to experiment with a curry or stew. These little changes can make a big difference, adding authenticity and depth to your meals.

Modern gadgets may save time, but traditional tools bring something far more valuable to the table: soul. They invite us to honour the ingredients, savour the process, and rediscover the art of slow, intentional cooking. So, dust off that mortar and pestle, grab a clay pot, and let the flavours of the past transform your present. Cooking isn't just about feeding the body; it's about feeding the spirit—and these tools make every bite a celebration.

The Science and Soul of Tadka

Tadka, the quintessential flourish in Indian cooking, is a sensory experience as much as a culinary technique. Also known as *tempering*, it is a deceptively simple act of heating spices in oil or ghee until they sizzle and release their aromatic essence. Yet, this humble process holds the power to transform the simplest of dishes into something extraordinary. It's where science meets soul, where tradition meets taste, and where a few crackling seeds can set the tone for an entire meal.

The magic of tadka lies in its ability to unlock the full potential of spices. The heat activates essential oils in the spices, intensifying their flavours and distributing them evenly throughout the dish. That teaspoon of hot, spiced oil isn't just a garnish; it's a culinary alchemy that elevates dals, curries, and even plain rice into works of art.

The Science Behind the Sizzle

At its core, tadka is about controlled chemistry. When spices meet hot oil or ghee, their essential oils are released, creating a burst of aroma and flavour. This step doesn't just enhance taste—it also aids digestion. Spices like cumin, mustard seeds, and fenugreek contain compounds that are activated by heat, making them easier for the body to process.

Take mustard seeds, for instance. When heated, they release a nutty aroma and their natural bitterness mellows, creating a balanced flavour profile. Cumin seeds, on the other hand, become warm and earthy, lending depth to dals and curries. Hing (*asafoetida*), a staple in many North and South Indian tadkas, releases its pungent, umami-rich aroma only when sautéed in hot oil.

The type of fat used—oil, ghee, or even coconut oil—also plays a crucial role. Ghee, with its high smoke point and nutty undertones, adds a richness that pairs beautifully with lentils and vegetables. Coconut oil, often used in South Indian cooking, brings a delicate sweetness that complements coastal flavours. The choice of fat isn't just about tradition; it's about balancing the dish's overall taste and texture.

The Soulful Ritual of Tadka

Beyond its scientific merit, tadka is a ritual steeped in tradition and sensory delight. It's the crescendo of the cooking process—the moment when the kitchen fills with the unmistakable aroma of sizzling spices, signaling that the meal is about to come alive. In many Indian households, tadka is an act of love, performed with precision and care.

There's something deeply satisfying about the sequence of events: the shimmer of hot oil, the pop of mustard seeds, the dance of curry leaves, and the hiss as chopped garlic or ginger hits the pan. The entire process is a symphony of sights, sounds, and smells. It's a moment of mindfulness, a pause to engage fully with the ingredients and the dish being prepared.

In many ways, tadka is storytelling. The choice of spices reflects the cook's regional roots, personal preferences, and even the occasion. A Punjabi *tadka* for dal might feature cumin and garlic, while a South Indian one for rasam leans heavily on mustard seeds, curry leaves, and dried red chillies. These variations are as diverse as the country itself, turning every tadka into a cultural narrative.

Tadka Across India

The beauty of tadka is its versatility—it adapts to every region and cuisine across India. In Bengal, for example, *phoron* (a mix of fennel, fenugreek, mustard, nigella, and cumin seeds) forms the backbone of tempering. The sizzling blend of spices adds complexity to dishes like *shukto* or *dal.*

In Gujarat, tadka often includes a touch of sweetness, with sugar or jaggery balanced by the heat of green chillies. This sweet-and-spicy tempering is a hallmark of Gujarati dals and *kadhi.*

In Karnataka, coconut oil is the fat of choice, lending a delicate flavour to tempering for dishes like *bisi bele bath* or *chitranna* (lemon rice). The crackle of curry leaves in hot oil is an unmistakable invitation to the table.

Beyond Lentils and Curries

While tadka is most commonly associated with dals and curries, its magic isn't limited to these staples. A tadka of mustard seeds, curry leaves, and red chillies transforms simple steamed rice into a fragrant delight. A garlic tadka poured over sautéed greens adds a burst of flavour to an otherwise plain dish. Even something as humble as yoghurt can be elevated with a tempering of mustard seeds, green chillies, and asafoetida, turning it into a zesty raita or a South Indian style pachadi.

The Joy of Experimentation

Tadka is forgiving, which makes it the perfect playground for culinary experimentation. You can try tempering spices in butter for a creamy dal makhani or use sesame oil for an East-Asian-inspired twist. Adding whole spices like cloves or cinnamon to your tempering can bring unexpected warmth and depth to otherwise straightforward recipes.

The timing of the tadka also offers room for creativity. While it's traditionally the finishing touch, some cooks incorporate it early in the process, using it to build the dish's foundation. Either way, the tadka's magic remains undeniable.

Tadka: A Tradition Worth Preserving

In a world of fast food and shortcuts, tadka reminds us to slow down and honour the ingredients we cook with. It's a celebration of simplicity, a testament to the idea that even the smallest things—like a teaspoon of hot oil and a handful of spices—can make a world of difference.

So, the next time you make a dal or curry, pause before you add that tadka. Watch the spices dance, listen to the sizzle, and breathe in the aroma. It's more than a cooking step; it's an act of love, a ritual, and a connection to centuries of culinary wisdom. With every crackle and hiss, tadka transforms not just the dish, but the entire cooking experience.

Fermentation: A Love Letter to Time

Fermentation is the culinary equivalent of slow magic, a process that turns the ordinary into the extraordinary with nothing more than time, patience, and a little bit of care. In the world of Indian cooking, fermentation isn't just a method—it's a love letter to flavours, nutrition, and tradition. From the tangy fluffiness of idlis to the deep complexity of pickles, fermentation has been an integral part of the Indian kitchen for centuries, connecting us to our roots and our taste buds in the most delightful way.

The beauty of fermentation lies in its simplicity. It's essentially a collaboration between nature and nurture, where beneficial bacteria and yeast work together to transform raw ingredients into something more nutritious, digestible, and delicious. All it takes is the right environment—a little warmth, a touch of moisture, and, most importantly, time. In a culture that often feels rushed, fermentation is a gentle reminder that good things really do come to those who wait.

Fermentation in Everyday Indian Food

Think of your favourite Indian dishes, and chances are, fermentation plays a starring role. South India's breakfast staples—idlis, dosas, and uttapams—wouldn't exist without the overnight fermentation of rice and urad dal batter. It's this natural leavening process that gives these dishes their light, airy texture and characteristic tang.

Then there's dahi, or yoghurt, arguably the most beloved fermented food in Indian households. Whether it's a cooling accompaniment to spicy curries, the base for creamy raita, or simply enjoyed on its own, yoghurt is a testament to the transformative power of fermentation. The live cultures in dahi not only enhance digestion but also make it a probiotic powerhouse long before the term became trendy.

Of course, no discussion of Indian fermentation would be complete without pickles. From the fiery mango achar of Punjab to the zesty lemon pickles of Gujarat, fermented pickles are as diverse as the country itself. These tangy delights are more than just condiments—they're culinary time capsules, capturing the essence of seasonal produce and preserving it for months, even years.

The Science of Fermentation

At its core, fermentation is a controlled process of microbial growth. Beneficial microorganisms—like lactic acid bacteria and yeast—feed on sugars and starches, breaking them down into acids, gases, and alcohol. This not only preserves the food but also enhances its flavour and nutritional value.

Take dosa batter, for example. When left to ferment, the naturally occurring bacteria in the soaked rice and dal release lactic acid, creating the batter's characteristic sourness. At the same time, the process increases the bioavailability of nutrients, making the dosa more nutritious than if the batter were used unfermented.

Similarly, fermentation in pickles not only intensifies their flavour but also produces beneficial compounds like probiotics, which support gut health. The same goes for yoghurt, where milk is transformed into a creamy, tangy superfood teeming with live cultures that aid digestion and boost immunity.

Time: The Unsung Hero of Fermentation

If there's one ingredient that defines fermentation, it's time. Fermentation cannot be rushed—it's a dance between patience and progress, where every hour adds depth to the final product. The tang of a perfectly fermented dosa batter or the complex spiciness of a well-aged pickle is a reward for respecting the process.

Yet, in a world where instant results are prized, fermentation feels almost radical. It asks us to slow down, to wait, and to trust that nature will do its work. And it never disappoints. The anticipation of tasting something that has taken days, weeks, or even months to perfect is a joy in itself—a small celebration of delayed gratification in an era of immediate satisfaction.

Fermentation as a Cultural Bridge

Fermentation isn't just about flavour; it's about tradition, connection, and community. Across India, the techniques and recipes for fermented foods are deeply regional, passed down through generations like heirlooms. In Tamil Nadu, the art of fermenting dosa batter is as central to family life as the morning filter coffee. In Himachal Pradesh, the unique *siddu* (a steamed bread made with fermented dough) showcases the versatility of fermentation in colder climates. And in Bengal, *kanji*—a probiotic-rich fermented rice water—is a reminder of how ancient methods continue to thrive in modern kitchens.

What's remarkable is how these regional practices are both deeply personal and universally relatable. They remind us that fermentation is more than just a technique—it's a way of life, rooted in the understanding that nature knows best when given the time and space to work its wonders.

A Modern Take on Fermentation

Even in today's fast-paced world, fermentation remains surprisingly accessible. With a few tweaks, anyone can incorporate this ancient art into their kitchen routine. The key is to start small: a batch of dosa batter for Sunday brunch, a jar of quick pickle to brighten up weekday meals, or even a pot of homemade yoghurt to replace store-bought options. These little steps are all it takes to rediscover the magic of fermentation.

And if you're worried about getting it wrong, remember this: fermentation is forgiving. It doesn't demand perfection—just a little care, a touch of warmth, and the willingness to wait. Like a good story, it unfolds in its own time, with each chapter adding complexity, flavour, and satisfaction.

Fermentation: A Taste of Tradition

In many ways, fermentation is the heart and soul of Indian cooking. It's a reminder of where we come from, of the Flavors and techniques that have shaped our culinary heritage. But it's also a promise of where we're going—a bridge between tradition and innovation, between the old ways and the new.

So, the next time you savour a fluffy idli, a tangy achar, or a bowl of creamy dahi, take a moment to appreciate the quiet magic that made it possible. Fermentation isn't just about transforming food; it's about transforming the way we think about time, patience, and the power of nature. And in that transformation, we find a connection to our past, a celebration of the present, and a little taste of the future.

Bringing Tradition to Modern Kitchens

Tradition and modernity often feel like opposites in the kitchen. One evokes images of slow-simmering pots, hand-ground spices, and recipes passed down through generations, while the other conjures gadgets, pre-packaged ingredients, and meals prepped in minutes. Yet, these two worlds are not mutually exclusive. In fact, blending the wisdom of traditional Indian cooking with the convenience of modern kitchens can create meals that are both soulful and efficient, honouring the past while embracing the present.

Indian cooking, in its essence, has always been about adaptability. For centuries, regional cuisines evolved based on the local produce, climate, and available tools. In the same way, today's kitchens can incorporate ancestral methods using the technology and time-saving devices we have at our disposal. It's not about replicating the past perfectly but about carrying its essence forward. With a little creativity, tradition can find a comfortable place in the fast-paced kitchens of today.

Rethinking Time in the Kitchen

One of the main challenges of traditional cooking is its perceived demand for time. Who has hours to slow-cook dal or grind masalas when juggling work, family, and everything in between? The good news is that modern tools can help without sacrificing the heart of the process. For instance, a pressure cooker is a perfect substitute for the hours traditionally spent simmering dals or curries on a low flame. It retains the depth of flavour while shaving hours off the cooking time. Similarly, slow cookers allow you to bring the magic of "low and slow" cooking into your routine with minimal hands-on effort. Let the pot do the work while you go about your day.

Another modern adaptation is batch cooking. Many traditional dishes—like dals, chutneys, and masalas—can be prepared in larger quantities and stored for later use. Freeze portions of cooked dal or pre-made masala bases in small containers, and you'll have the building blocks for a wholesome, home-cooked meal ready to go. This approach respects the soul of traditional cooking while making it feasible for a busy schedule.

Traditional Tools, Modern Applications

While modern gadgets have their place, there's a certain charm and effectiveness to traditional tools that's hard to replicate. Take the humble mortar and pestle, for example. Grinding spices by hand releases essential oils that create a depth of flavour unmatched by pre-ground powders or even electric grinders. Yet, you don't have to grind every spice blend manually—reserve this technique for special recipes or when you're seeking that extra burst of aroma and freshness.

Clay pots, once a mainstay of Indian kitchens, can feel like relics in today's world of stainless steel and non-stick cookware. Yet their ability to retain heat and add an earthy flavour to dishes like biryanis, curries, and even simple rice is unparalleled. If sourcing or maintaining a clay pot feels daunting, cast iron or ceramic cookware can offer a similar experience, bridging the gap between tradition and convenience.

Even rolling pins (belans) and boards for making flatbreads like rotis or parathas retain their value in modern kitchens. While store-bought options are tempting, there's something deeply satisfying about rolling out your own bread, connecting your hands to the dough in a way that feels almost meditative.

Reviving Lost Practices

Some aspects of traditional cooking have been all but forgotten in the rush of modern life, yet they're surprisingly easy to bring back. Take fermentation, for example. The art of fermenting dosa batter or making homemade yoghurt (dahi) might seem like an unnecessary effort when pre-made options are so readily available, but the rewards go beyond taste. Fermentation not only enhances flavour but also improves digestion and adds probiotics to your diet. By carving out a little time to let nature work its magic, you'll rediscover the joy of nurturing food from start to finish.

Similarly, tempering, or *tadka*, is a quick, impactful way to inject traditional flavour into even the simplest dishes. By heating oil or ghee and infusing it with spices like cumin, mustard seeds, or curry leaves, you can transform plain lentils, rice, or vegetables into something vibrant and flavourful. The beauty of *tadka* is its adaptability—you can add it to pre-cooked dishes or even incorporate it into non-traditional recipes, like soups or pasta, for a subtle Indian twist.

Celebrating Local and Seasonal Ingredients

Traditional Indian cooking has always been grounded in seasonality. Mangoes in summer, mustard greens in winter, and a myriad of pulses and grains year-round—these were the rhythms that shaped the meals of our ancestors. Today, it's easy to lose sight of this connection in the globalised world of supermarkets, where everything seems to be in season all the time.

However, embracing local and seasonal produce doesn't just honour tradition—it's also more sustainable and often tastier. Seasonal fruits and vegetables are harvested at their peak, offering better flavour and nutrition. Shopping at local markets or sourcing directly from farmers can be a small but meaningful way to reconnect with this philosophy. Plus, it's a creative challenge to design meals around what's available, just as our ancestors did.

Infusing Tradition into Everyday Meals

You don't have to cook a three-hour meal to embrace traditional methods. Sometimes, small touches can make all the difference. Adding freshly ground spices to your curry, fermenting a simple batter for the weekend, or using leftover rice to make a quick lemon rice with a *tadka* can bring a sense of heritage into your cooking without upending your routine.

Even "fusion" dishes can carry the spirit of tradition. Imagine blending Indian flavours with global techniques—like adding garam masala to a roasted vegetable soup or using curry leaves in a pasta dish. These playful nods to tradition keep cooking fresh and fun while celebrating the adaptability of Indian cuisine.

The Joy of Cooking with Intention

At its heart, bringing tradition into modern kitchens isn't just about recipes or tools—it's about mindset. Traditional cooking invites us to slow down, to pay attention, and to find joy in the process as much as the result. It's about valuing the journey of a dish, from chopping and grinding to simmering and serving, as a form of connection to our heritage and ourselves.

In a world that often prioritises convenience over care, these small acts of intention—whether it's taking the time to temper spices or letting a pot of dal simmer just a little longer—are a quiet rebellion. They remind us that food is not just fuel but a reflection of culture, family, and love.

So, the next time you step into your kitchen, consider adding a touch of tradition to your routine. Roll out that roti, temper those spices, or let a dish take its time to cook. In doing so, you're not just preparing a meal—you're keeping alive a legacy that has been passed down through generations. And in every bite, you'll taste not just the flavours of the past, but the promise of something timeless and enduring.

Chapter 9

Sweet Satisfaction – Desserts That Won't Sabotage Your Health

Why Indian Sweets Are So Special

Indian sweets, or **mithai**, hold a cherished place in our culinary heritage. They're more than just food—they're expressions of love, celebration, and community. Whether it's the laddoos (sweetened flour balls) made by a grandmother's hands or the perfect rosogulla (spongy syrup-soaked dumplings) savoured on a trip to Kolkata, these treats are steeped in nostalgia and meaning. Across the vast cultural landscape of India, sweets have woven themselves into the fabric of life, marking every festival, milestone, and shared moment with their rich flavours and textures.

Each region boasts its signature treats, crafted with ingredients that reflect its geography and traditions. In the southern states, coconut and jaggery (unrefined cane sugar) dominate, creating heavenly modaks (steamed rice dumplings) and barfis (fudge-like squares) that transport you to palm-fringed shores. Rajasthan's ghewar (honeycomb-shaped dessert), with its delicate, almost architectural structure, celebrates the art of craftsmanship as much as indulgence. Meanwhile, Punjab's ghee-laden pinnis (nut and flour energy balls), bursting with dried fruits and warmth, are winter's sweet armour against the biting cold. These desserts are not just recipes; they're edible snapshots of a place and its people.

What makes Indian sweets so special is the attention to detail in their preparation. Take, for instance, Bengal's sandesh—a deceptively simple confection of chenna and sugar. It's an exercise in balance and finesse, requiring the perfect ratio of moisture and sweetness to achieve its melt-in-the-mouth texture. Similarly, Mysore pak (gram flour fudge), a ghee-soaked marvel, demands a precise dance of timing and heat to transform humble ingredients into a dessert that feels like silk on the palate.

And then there's the sheer variety. No single occasion calls for the same mithai twice. Diwali lights up with kaju katlis (cashew fudge) and gulab jamuns (fried dough balls in syrup), while Holi bursts forth with gujiyas (sweet pastry pockets) and malpuas (syrup-soaked pancakes). Even daily life is sweetened with dishes like suji halwa (semolina pudding), often served as **prasadam** (food offered in religious rituals) in temples, connecting people to the divine through the language of flavours. In India, no celebration is complete without something sweet, and every bite tells a story—of seasons, of rituals, and of the people who first brought these recipes to life.

At the heart of Indian sweets are ingredients that are as symbolic as they are delicious. Jaggery, for instance, is not just a sweetener but a link to the earth, minimally processed and rich with mineral-laden sweetness. It lends its caramel-like depth to til ke laddoos (sesame seed balls) and gud ka halwa (jaggery pudding), adding a rustic charm that white sugar simply can't match. Coconut, in its myriad forms—grated, dried, or as milk—offers creamy decadence in sweets like payasam (sweetened milk dessert) and naralachi vadi (coconut fudge), especially beloved in coastal cuisines. Even spices like cardamom and saffron elevate sweets beyond their ingredients, infusing them with warmth, aroma, and a touch of luxury.

However, the richness of these sweets often comes with a trade-off. The heavy use of ghee (clarified butter), sugar, and frying techniques has made some of these treats a challenge for modern, health-conscious lifestyles. (After all, no one wants to feel like a gulab jamun rolling home after Diwali dinner.) But even within these traditional recipes lies the potential for balance. Ancient wisdom always celebrated moderation, and the ingredients themselves—rich in nutrients and packed with natural energy—are a testament to how sweets can be both indulgent and nourishing.

Indian sweets also embody the art of mindful eating. The best mithai is made in small batches, savoured slowly, and appreciated for its intricate flavours and textures. A single bite of well-made peda (milk fudge) or boondi laddoo (tiny pearl-shaped gram flour balls in syrup) has the power to transport you, offering satisfaction that lingers long after the sweetness fades. This quality makes mithai a treat worth celebrating, one that doesn't demand excess but rewards attention and appreciation.

In a world increasingly drawn to quick fixes and shortcuts, Indian sweets remain an act of devotion. They're crafted with patience, often requiring long hours of stirring, simmering, and perfecting. From the golden bubbles of jalebi (crispy syrup-soaked spirals) batter frying to the rhythmic rolling of laddoos, the process is as much a part of the experience as the end result. These sweets remind us to slow down, to savour the process as much as the taste, and to find joy in creating something that brings happiness to others.

Finally, the joy of Indian sweets lies not just in their taste but in their ability to bring people together. Sharing a plate of kheer (rice pudding) at a family gathering or passing around a box of kaju katlis at work creates connections that transcend words. These moments remind us of that food, especially sweets, is about more than nourishment—it's about celebrating life, love, and the small joys that make every day a little sweeter.

Making Sweets That Don't Sabotage Your Health

Indian sweets, with their rich flavours and indulgent textures, are undeniably tempting. But let's be honest—most mithai recipes come with a health price tag that includes copious amounts of ghee, sugar, and deep frying. While a laddoo here or a gulab jamun there is worth every calorie, a steady diet of these can quickly make you feel less like a festive spirit and more like a stuffed paratha. The good news? Enjoying your favourite desserts doesn't have to come at the expense of your health—or your taste buds. With a little creativity and a few smart swaps, you can create sweets that are just as satisfying but far kinder to your waistline (and your energy levels).

One simple but transformative change is the substitution of refined sugar with jaggery or dates. Jaggery, with its rich caramel undertones, brings a depth of flavour that plain white sugar could never hope to achieve. Think about til ke laddoos made with jaggery—suddenly, the nuttiness of sesame seeds comes alive in a way that's earthy and indulgent. Similarly, dates, often called nature's candy, can be blended into a paste and used to sweeten desserts like halwa or barfi, adding a chewy texture and natural sweetness while cutting out refined sugar altogether. These sweeteners don't just improve the taste; they also pack a nutritional punch, offering minerals like iron and potassium that refined sugar completely lacks.

Then there are the unsung heroes of healthier mithai: nuts, seeds, and whole grains. Ingredients like almonds, pistachios, cashews, and sesame seeds can lend richness and crunch while adding protein, healthy fats, and fibre. Imagine a laddoo made with ground almonds, jaggery, and toasted sesame seeds—it's indulgent, filling, and loaded with nutrients. Similarly, whole grains like ragi (millet), oats, or barley can add a nutty flavour and wholesome texture to sweets. Ragi halwa, for instance, is a great example of how whole grains can transform a classic dish. Its earthy flavour pairs beautifully with cardamom and ghee, and it keeps you satisfied far longer than its semolina-based counterpart.

Of course, let's not forget coconut, the unsung champion of Indian desserts. From payasam to modaks, coconut—in its grated, dried, or milk form—brings a natural sweetness and creamy texture that's utterly irresistible. The best part? It's packed with healthy fats and has a relatively low glycaemic index, making it a fantastic choice for those looking to avoid sugar spikes. Coconut laddoos made with jaggery, for instance, deliver all the richness and sweetness of traditional recipes but feel lighter and more energising. It's like finding a dessert that loves you back.

Another area where traditional recipes can be lightened up is the fat content. While ghee is non-negotiable in many mithai recipes for its unmatched flavour, reducing the quantity slightly or supplementing it with healthier fats like nut butters or coconut oil can make a big difference. Cashew or almond butter, for example, can add a creamy texture to barfis or halwas without relying solely on ghee. The key is balance—use ghee for flavour, but let other fats carry some of the richness.

Portion control also plays a starring role in healthier sweet indulgence. Let's face it: Indian sweets are often served in oversized portions that are impossible to resist (we've all had that "just one more gulab jamun" moment). But smaller servings, enjoyed mindfully, can be just as satisfying. Instead of a massive bowl of kheer, try a petite cup garnished with toasted nuts and a few strands of saffron. A single, well-made kaju katli can feel far more indulgent when savoured slowly than a plateful wolfed down in minutes. Mindful eating isn't about restraint; it's about maximising the joy of every bite.

The secret to healthier Indian desserts lies not in stripping them of their essence but in enhancing their best qualities. Spices like cardamom, saffron, and cinnamon, for example, are already a cornerstone of mithai, but they can do much of the flavour heavy lifting when sugar and fat are dialled back. A touch of saffron dissolved in warm milk can elevate a simple kheer into something divine, while a sprinkle of freshly ground cardamom transforms any dessert into an aromatic masterpiece. These natural flavour boosters let the true essence of the ingredients shine, so you're not just tasting sugar or ghee—you're experiencing the layered complexity of traditional recipes.

Let's talk practicalities: how do you actually go about reimagining mithai for modern, health-conscious kitchens? Start by choosing one or two elements of a recipe to tweak. For instance, if you're making halwa, consider swapping half the sugar for jaggery or using less ghee than the recipe demands. If you're whipping up laddoos, try incorporating ground nuts or seeds to replace some of the flour or sugar. The key is to experiment with small changes and taste as you go—after all, Indian desserts are all about the perfect balance of flavours.

And don't underestimate the power of presentation. Healthier desserts, when plated beautifully, feel just as indulgent as their traditional counterparts. A handful of toasted pistachios, a dusting of dried rose petals, or a drizzle of saffron-infused syrup can make even the simplest mithai feel luxurious. Remember, we eat with our eyes first, and a little extra effort in presentation can make your healthier sweets feel as celebratory as their more indulgent cousins.

Ultimately, the goal isn't to make Indian sweets "healthy" in the clinical sense—it's to create desserts that make you feel good, both while eating and afterward. The joy of mithai lies in its ability to bring people together, to mark special moments, and to satisfy cravings in the most delightful way possible. With a few thoughtful adjustments, you can keep all the magic of traditional recipes while making them a little kinder to your body and soul. So go ahead— roll up those laddoos, stir that halwa, and drizzle that kheer with love. A little creativity is all it takes to sweeten your life, guilt-free.

Healthier Ingredients for Indian Sweets

When it comes to Indian sweets, the ingredients are the stars of the show. They're the foundation of each mithai, bringing the richness, sweetness, and complexity that make these desserts so beloved. But while traditional recipes often rely on sugar and ghee to do the heavy lifting, a new cast of healthier ingredients is ready to take the spotlight. These swaps aren't about making your mithai taste like health food—they're about creating sweets that are just as indulgent but with a little more balance. After all, what's better than enjoying your favourite desserts and knowing they're working with you, not against you?

Jaggery is the undisputed queen of alternative sweeteners. Think of it as sugar's cooler, more sophisticated cousin. Unlike white sugar, which is stripped of everything but sweetness, jaggery retains its mineral-rich charm. It's earthy, caramel-like, and has a depth of flavour that sugar simply can't match. From til ke laddoos to gud ka halwa, jaggery doesn't just sweeten—it transforms. Imagine biting into a gajak (crispy sesame brittle) made with jaggery instead of sugar: it's not just dessert, it's a warm hug in edible form. Plus, jaggery has a lower glycaemic index, which means it's kinder to your blood sugar levels. It's like upgrading from a rickety autorickshaw to a smooth electric ride—still fun, but much easier on the system.

Dates and figs are the health-conscious sweet tooth's best friends. These natural sweeteners are packed with fibre, nutrients, and antioxidants. A single medjool date is like a little bomb of caramel, ready to explode with flavour in your mouth. Blend a few dates into a paste, and you've got the perfect base for laddoos, barfis, or even a cheeky no-bake dessert ball. Figs, with their chewy texture and subtle crunch of seeds, are equally magical. They pair beautifully with nuts and spices, turning a simple sweet into a textural delight. Think of these fruits as nature's way of saying, "Here's dessert, but make it nutritious."

Nuts and seeds are the unsung heroes of healthier mithai. They're like the side characters in a film who end up stealing the show. Almonds, pistachios, cashews, sesame seeds—each brings its unique flair. Cashews offer creaminess, pistachios bring a hint of luxury, and sesame seeds deliver crunch and warmth. Nuts are high in protein and healthy fats, meaning they help you feel full and satisfied with smaller portions. Meanwhile, seeds like chia or flax can sneak in extra fibre and omega-3s. The best part? They're versatile. Whether you're blending cashews into a paste for creamy kheer or rolling laddoos in sesame seeds, nuts and seeds are the ultimate multi-taskers.

Coconut, in all its glorious forms, is a game-changer for healthier Indian sweets. Fresh coconut, desiccated coconut, coconut milk—each has a way of adding richness without feeling heavy. Coconut laddoos are the perfect example: creamy, sweet, and satisfying without the sugar overload. And let's not forget coconut milk's role in payasam or kheer. It's like inviting a tropical breeze to your dessert table. Plus, coconut has a natural sweetness and is low on the glycaemic index, making it a smart choice for those who want to enjoy their mithai without worrying about sugar spikes.

Whole grains are the underdog of Indian sweets, quietly bringing their nutty flavours and fibre to the party. Ragi (finger millet), oats, and even barley can transform a dish without overpowering its traditional essence. Ragi flour in halwas or laddoos adds a subtle earthiness that pairs beautifully with jaggery and spices. Meanwhile, oats can sneak into kheer or barfi recipes, adding chewiness and fibre while reducing the reliance on refined flour. Whole grains don't just make desserts healthier—they add a satisfying depth that makes each bite more memorable.

And what's an Indian dessert without the magic of spices? Cardamom, saffron, cinnamon, nutmeg—these little powerhouses can elevate a dish from sweet to sublime. Cardamom, with its floral notes, is the backbone of kheer and gulab jamun. Saffron, those precious golden strands, add both flavour and a sense of occasion. A dash of cinnamon can bring warmth to halwa, while nutmeg whispers of festive indulgence. Spices allow you to dial down the sweetness while still delivering that unforgettable burst of flavour. Plus, they come with their own health benefits—cardamom aids digestion, saffron boosts mood, and cinnamon helps regulate blood sugar. It's like having a dessert that doubles as a wellness retreat.

Of course, there's ghee. Ah, ghee—the liquid gold of Indian cooking. While its calorie count can make you break out in a sweat just thinking about it, ghee is actually not the villain it's sometimes made out to be. When used in moderation, ghee adds a richness and aroma that's hard to replicate. But here's the trick: you don't need as much as you think. A teaspoon or two can go a long way in laddoos or halwas. For an extra health boost, you can pair ghee with nut butters or coconut oil, striking a balance between tradition and modernity.

When reimagining traditional sweets, the goal isn't to strip them of their identity but to highlight their best features. Small tweaks—like reducing sugar, adding fibre, or balancing ghee with lighter fats—can make a big difference. And the beauty of Indian mithai is that it's inherently rich in textures and flavours, so a little goes a long way. By swapping in ingredients like jaggery, nuts, and whole grains, you can create desserts that feel indulgent while being nourishing. It's not about saying no to sweets; it's about saying yes to desserts that make you feel good in every way.

With these ingredient upgrades, mithai doesn't have to be a rare indulgence reserved for festivals or cheat days. It can be a part of your everyday life, offering comfort, joy, and just a little bit of nostalgia—all without sabotaging your health goals. So next time you're rolling laddoos or stirring halwa, don't hesitate to experiment with these simple swaps. After all, tradition isn't about staying stuck in the past—it's about keeping the best parts alive while embracing the present.

PART IV

Final Reflections

Chapter 10

Epilogue: Cooking with Confidence and Joy

The kitchen is more than just a space for cooking—it's a canvas for creativity, a hub of tradition, and a stage for moments that connect us to family, culture, and ourselves. As we've journeyed through the diverse and rich world of Indian cooking, one truth emerges: food is more than sustenance. It's an expression of love, a celebration of heritage, and a way to nourish both body and soul.

Cooking can feel intimidating at times, especially when faced with complex recipes, unfamiliar techniques, or the fear of not getting it "right." But here's the secret: there's no perfect way to cook. Whether it's a perfectly layered biryani or a quick stir-fry thrown together on a busy weeknight, every dish you create is a testament to your effort, your love for good food, and your willingness to try. Cooking isn't about perfection—it's about connection, creativity, and joy.

Indian cuisine, with its symphony of spices, layers of flavours, and rich traditions, can sometimes feel overwhelming. The towering masala shelves, the precise timing of a tadka, the slow alchemy of a simmering curry—these are skills honed over generations, yes, but they're also acts of experimentation and discovery. The joy of cooking comes from the process itself, from that moment when the aroma of frying onions fills the kitchen or when you take the first taste of a dish that's finally come together. It's a practice as much as it is an art, and the more you lean into it, the more rewarding it becomes.

One of the greatest joys of Indian cooking is its adaptability. It's a cuisine that invites personal touches and celebrates individuality. No two aloo parathas are ever the same—not because one is better, but because each carries the signature of the person rolling it. Whether you prefer more chilli in your curry or like your laddoos on the smaller side, Indian food embraces those differences. That's the beauty of this culinary tradition: it offers guidelines, not rules, leaving room for your creativity and intuition to shine.

Cooking with confidence means embracing that freedom. It's about trusting your senses—smelling the spices as they toast, tasting the curry as it simmers, adjusting seasoning until it feels just right. Confidence doesn't come from knowing every technique or having a perfectly stocked pantry; it comes from the willingness to try, to fail, and to learn. It comes from understanding that mistakes are part of the process, whether it's burning the first roti or accidentally adding too much salt to a dal. Every misstep is a step closer to mastering the art, and every dish—flawed or flawless—is a step closer to discovering your unique style in the kitchen.

Joy, on the other hand, comes from remembering why we cook in the first place. Food has always been about more than just eating. It's about gathering around a table with loved ones, about sharing stories over a steaming pot of chai, about finding comfort in a bowl of khichdi on a rainy day. The act of cooking is, in itself, an act of care—whether it's for others or for yourself. It's a way of saying, "You matter, and so does this moment." The most joyful cooking happens when we let go of the pressure to impress and focus instead on the happiness it brings, both to those who eat and to the one who cooks.

As you move forward in your culinary journey, remember that Indian cooking is as much about the experience as it is about the result. The sizzle of spices hitting hot oil, the rhythmic rolling of dough, the heady aroma of a masala being ground—all of these are moments to savour. Cooking isn't just about the final dish; it's about the laughter shared in the kitchen, the memories stirred up by a familiar smell, and the satisfaction of creating something with your own hands.

If there's one takeaway from this journey, let it be this: cooking is for everyone. You don't need to be an expert to start, nor do you need the fanciest tools or the rarest ingredients. What matters is the intention, the effort, and the willingness to try. Whether you're crafting a multi-layered biryani or making a simple dal with rice, every meal cooked with care is a celebration of what food represents—connection, creativity, and love.

So go ahead, stock your spice shelf with the blends that make your heart sing. Experiment with recipes from regions you've never visited. Slow down to simmer a curry, or whip up a quick stir-fry when time is tight. And don't forget to sprinkle a little joy into every dish you make, because at the end of the day, the best ingredient in any meal is the love that goes into it.

Cooking with confidence and joy isn't about mastering every recipe or nailing every dish—it's about finding the pleasure in the process, the meaning in the moments, and the courage to keep trying. So, tie on your apron, grab that ladle, and step into your kitchen with the knowledge that every meal you create is a celebration of tradition, innovation, and most importantly, you.

Acknowledgments, References and Resources

References and Resources

For those interested in delving deeper into the topics of traditional cooking methods, health benefits of spices, and safe cookware choices, here's a comprehensive list of books, journals, and trusted sources. This collection provides a balanced mix of scholarly insights, practical guides, and culturally rich narratives.

Books on Indian Cooking and Culture

1. **The Indian Cookery Book by Krishna Gopal Dubey**

   A timeless guide to authentic Indian cooking techniques and recipes.

2. **Indian Food: A Historical Companion by K. T. Achaya**

   Explores the origins and evolution of Indian cuisine, including its unique ingredients and cooking styles.

3. **The Flavour Matrix by James Briscione and Brooke Parkhurst**

   A fascinating guide to the science of flavour pairings, helping readers experiment with traditional and modern ingredients.

4. **Healing Spices: How to Use 50 Everyday and Exotic Spices to Boost Health and Beat Disease by Bharat B. Aggarwal**

    practical resource for understanding the medicinal properties of commonly used spices.

5. **On Food and Cooking: The Science and Lore of the Kitchen by Harold McGee**

    Offers scientific insights into cookware materials and their interaction with food, enhancing your cooking experience.

Journals and Research Studies

1. **Journal of Food Science and Technology**

    Features research on traditional Indian cooking methods, ingredient safety, and cookware impact.

2. **Journal of Ethnic Foods**

    Highlights cultural significance and the health benefits of traditional Indian food practices.

3. **International Journal of Food Sciences and Nutrition**

    Includes studies on nutrient retention, cookware material effects, and safe cooking techniques.

4. **Environmental Health Perspectives**

    Reports on the health risks associated with non-stick cookware and chemicals like PTFE and PFOA.

5. **Journal of Agricultural and Food Chemistry**

    Discusses the effects of cookware on nutrient preservation and the safety of food.

Cookware Safety and Guidance

1. **Food Safety and Standards Authority of India (FSSAI)**

   Offers guidelines on food safety and recommended cookware materials for Indian households.

2. **FDA (U.S. Food and Drug Administration)**

   Provides insights into non-stick cookware safety and chemical concerns.

3. **European Food Safety Authority (EFSA)**

   Covers European standards for food-contact materials, including ceramic-coated cookware.

4. **Indian Council of Medical Research (ICMR)**

   Studies the safety of cookware options like cast iron, stainless steel, and clay pots.

5. **National Institute of Nutrition (India)**

   Researches the impact of cookware materials on health and provides practical recommendations for Indian kitchens.

Websites and Recipe Resources

1. **Sanjeev Kapoor's Kitchen**

   A treasure trove of recipes, cookware advice, and tips on incorporating traditional techniques with modern tools.

2. **Tarla Dalal's Website**

   Features a vast range of health-conscious recipes and guidance on cookware choices for Indian cuisine.

3. **America's Test Kitchen**

Offers scientific explanations and reviews of cookware materials, including cast iron and stainless steel.

4. **Cook's Illustrated**

Provides comprehensive tests on cookware performance and its suitability for various cooking methods.

5. **Hebbars Kitchen**

Short video tutorials that incorporate Indian cooking traditions with easy-to-find ingredients and tools.

Cookware-Specific Reading

1. **The Science of Cooking by Dr. Stuart Farrimond**

Answers common questions about cookware and explains their effect on cooking outcomes.

2. **Ceramic Coated Cookware and Health Concerns**

Articles discussing the pros and cons of ceramic coatings and how to select safe options.

3. **Cast Iron Cooking for Dummies by Tracy Barr**

A beginner's guide to using, seasoning, and maintaining cast iron cookware for healthier, tastier meals.

4. **Indian Health Ministry's Advisory on Safe Cookware**

Recommendations for stainless steel, cast iron, and clay cookware options.

Spices and Traditional Cooking

1. **Healing Foods: Cooking for Better Health by Vasant Lad**

A guide to Ayurvedic cooking, blending traditional Indian practices with health-conscious recipes.

2. **Masala Lab: The Science of Indian Cooking by Krish Ashok**

    Combines humour with science to demystify Indian cooking techniques and spice use.

3. **The Flavor Thesaurus by Niki Segnit**

    A creative take on flavour combinations, inspiring new twists on traditional recipes.

4. **Ancient Indian Kitchen by Lathika George**

    Chronicles traditional cooking techniques and tools, including mortar and pestle and clay pot cooking.

Acknowledgments

Writing this book has been as much a journey as cooking itself—filled with experiments, laughs, the occasional mishap, and a lot of love. I want to thank each person who's inspired, supported, and shared this passion for food, family, and flavour with me.

To my family, who have been my toughest critics and biggest cheerleaders, thank you for every taste test, every "maybe a bit more salt," and every story shared over meals. Your love and patience made this book possible.

To friends and mentors who encouraged me to turn a simple love for cooking into a guide for others, thank you for your endless support and insight. And to the readers who've joined me on this journey, thank you for trusting me to share a piece of your kitchen and your table. I hope this book brings you as much joy and inspiration as it has brought me.

Here's to meals made with love, laughter, and just the right amount of spice.

www.ingramcontent.com/pod-product-compliance
Lightning Source LLC
Chambersburg PA
CBHW021438150726
47989CB00001B/288